THE DEVELOPMENT OF PEOPLES

International Jesuit Network for Development

The Development of Peoples: Challenges for Today and Tomorrow

ESSAYS TO MARK THE FORTIETH ANNIVERSARY OF
POPULORUM PROGRESSIO

the columba press

First published in 2007 by
the columba press
55A Spruce Avenue, Stillorgan Industrial Park,
Blackrock, Co Dublin

Cover design: www.artisan.ie
Origination by The Columba Press
Printed in Ireland by ColourBooks Ltd, Dublin

ISBN 978 1 85607 574 9

Note: The views expressed in this book are those of the authors and do not necessarily reflect the views of either the Jesuit Centre for Faith and Justice or the International Jesuit Network for Development.

Table of Contents

CONCLUSIONS

APPENDIX

Preface

The International Jesuit Network for Development (IJND) is a global network of Jesuit social centres. It exists to facilitate and promote new ways for Jesuits, their colleagues, and their institutions to work with other organisations and social movements to pursue a goal that is simply stated. That goal is to realise the integral human development for each and every person in community, and universal global solidarity through justice for all and care of the earth.

Such a goal is easily stated but the practical task of realising it is rightly described as a struggle. While progress is made on some fronts, many problems remain and new ones emerge. The struggle for the just development of all peoples requires us to mobilise the combined intellectual, social, cultural, political, moral and religious resources at our disposal. The millions of people who, because of global inequalities, live in hunger and abject poverty, are displaced or in need of refuge, suffer preventable diseases, and die preventable deaths, call out to us to remain concerned, focused, and committed to change.

This is often not easy – some of the challenges even seem insurmountable. It requires a vision of humanity and a vision of development that can inspire, guide and sustain action. For many the encyclical letter of Pope Paul Vl, *Populorum Progressio*, has helped shape and maintain such a vision for over four decades. The encyclical's unequivocal statement of support for the poor, its clear call to action, and its vision of human development, continue to inspire and guide responses to some of the most pressing problems facing humanity today.

IJND decided that the 40th anniversary of the publication of *Populorum Progressio* was an opportune time to invite experts and activists from around the world to reflect on the encyclical's enduring relevance to the most pressing development challenges of the present day. *The Development of Peoples: Challenges for Today and Tomorrow* brings together these reflections on issues across the development spectrum. Such issues include poverty, debt, trade, peace and conflict, human rights, globalis-ation, HIV/AIDS, gender inequality, the environment, and mig-ration.

It is appropriate to celebrate and mark this anniversary of *Populorum Progressio* and the efforts that it has inspired. However, as one reads *Populorum Progressio* and the essays in this book, the most appropriate way of commemorating the an-niversary of the encyclical must be a re-doubling of our efforts to work for the development of all peoples, in line with the call to action of *Populorum Progressio*.

This book would not have been possible without the efforts and cooperation of so many people. IJND would like to acknowl-edge the work of the initial editorial team – Peter Henriot SJ, Jim Hug SJ, Tony O'Riordan SJ and Eugene Quinn – who developed and refined the scope of this project. It is also necessary to thank them for using their persuasive powers to enlist the cooperation of the contributors. IJND would like to thank all those who took time within already busy schedules to write the contributions that appear in this book. In addition, IJND is enormously grate-ful to the Board and staff of the Jesuit Centre for Faith and Justice in Dublin for coordinating this project, and in particular for arranging and preparing the essays for publication. Particular gratitude is owing to Walt Kilroy, Jesuit Solidarity Scholar at the Jesuit Centre for Faith and Justice, for assembling and editing the material. In addition, IJND wishes to acknowl-edge the editing assistance of Margaret Burns and Tony O'Riordan SJ, also of the Jesuit Centre in Dublin. Thanks for help with translation are due to Brendan McManus SJ, Nicole Stapff, and Philip Endean SJ. The support and assistance of Dorothy Ní Uigín at the copy-editing stage and Bruce Bradley SJ, Máire Ní Chearbhaill and Joe Palmisano at the proof-reading stage proved invaluable in preparing the book for publication. IJND would also like to thank Padhraig Nolan of Artisan Visual Communication for the cover design, and The Columba Press – in particular Seán O Boyle – for the encouragement and support provided at several stages in the production of this publication.

Foreword

What inspires us to act for change? What informs and supports our vision of a more just world? There are many sources, both old and new, but it is especially noteworthy to look again at sources that continue to inspire action for a more just world. While *Populorum Progressio* springs from the Catholic tradition, the core values of justice, solidarity, and the protection of the weak from the strong are shared across religions, cultures and even time.

This document has proved a catalyst for action among many Catholics and others. I have been privileged to witness this action first hand. During my five-year term as UN High Commissioner for Human Rights I came to know many Justice and Peace groups that are part of a global network of human rights 'eyes and ears', drawing attention to hidden conflicts and situations of extreme injustice. Agencies such as Trócaire under the direction of Justin Kilcullen give effect to the vision of *Populorum Progressio*, translating solidarity expressed by ordinary citizens in Ireland into practical life-giving measures in some of the poorest parts of the world.

At the Social Forum in Nairobi in January 2007 I saw this activism in practice again, and I was pleased to participate in a session organised by the umbrella group CIDSE (*Coopération Internationale pour le Développement et la Solidarité*), that brought together a wide range of Catholic and other Christian agencies, and that focused on problems caused to local communities by extractive industries.

Over the years, and in discussions with Enda McDonagh, I have been aware of – and have greatly valued – the work being done on HIV / AIDS by the Catholic Agency for Overseas Development (CAFOD) and the networks working on this issue at grassroots level such as the African Jesuit AIDS Network and the Sisters in Africa Network. I often found, with pride, that where there was deep trauma after conflict there were priests, nuns and other aid workers, often with Irish accents, and a practical sense of humour, working with communities to protect them, and to begin the process of rebuilding fragile lives.

For much of my life I have been engaged in advocacy, seeking to tackle inequality and injustice and often found that some of my natural allies have been friends in the Catholic and Protestant ministry and other religious traditions. There are clear links between my preoccupation with holding governments accountable for implementing human rights and a focus on spiritual values. It is reflected in the first sentence of Article 1 of the *Universal Declaration of Human Rights*, which proclaims that 'All human beings are born free and equal in dignity and rights.' How appropriate it is to place dignity before rights, since dignity encompasses all the components of self-respect and inner spirituality, that sense of values and worth that are part of a person's identity. Listening to a family living in absolute poverty, it is this lack they speak of: the lack of self-respect, the indignity and humiliation of a refugee camp, the invisibility of being homeless, the helplessness in the face of violence, including violence caused by those in uniform who should protect. *Populorum Progressio* shares this emphasis on human dignity, which is translated into a pithy understanding of development as 'the transition from less than human conditions to truly human ones'.

On the 40th anniversary of the publication of *Populorum Progressio*, the authors in this book take the opportunity to bring the reader deeper into their worldview. They seek to recover the vision and goals set out 40 years ago. This book is not a journey down roads of nostalgia, however, because the authors look at the inspiration offered through the lens of response – they not only recall the vision and goals of *Populorum Progressio*, but they ask how we, as a global family, have fared in realising that vision and achieving these goals.

It is sobering to reflect that, like the 1948 *Universal Declaration of Human Rights*, many of the challenges raised in *Populorum Progressio* are still relevant – and radical. Its powerful message about justice, responsibility, and our relations with each other is still needed in today's unjust world. Its analysis of what this means for the social, political and economic systems we have created is vital if we are to be effective in shaping the world.

While not widely acknowledged when *Populorum Progressio* was written in 1967, one of the key processes underlying the changing relationships in the world is what we now call globalisation. Globalisation has many aspects, both positive and negative, and the term is sometimes used to mean completely different things. However, the growing interconnectedness and interdependence of our world – and the dominance of certain ideas and systems – marks a radical change in our relationships with each other.

Populorum Progressio provides a basis for shaping those relationships, and for deciding what kind of globalisation we bring about, by dealing with issues such as trade, justice, and the distribution of wealth. Do we want a globalisation that enriches all of us in an exchange of cultures, ideas and fairly-traded goods? Or one that sees a homogenisation of ideas and the imposition, by the powerful, of dehumanising economic systems?

The rapid changes brought about by technology and innovation are both a threat and an opportunity. New solutions and possibilities are created, but these are only options for those who can afford to pay for them, initially at least, and solutions tend to be found for problems which afflict the wealthy – like pharmaceutical products for diseases of the rich, rather than those illnesses that claim millions of lives in the developing world. Technological innovation, therefore, is not a value-free process: *Populorum Progressio* challenges us to bring an ethical consideration to the debate.

While many of the challenges raised in *Populorum Progressio* are still relevant 40 years on, there are some significant issues today that were not mentioned. An obvious one is the dangerous and perhaps irreversible changes being made to our climate, which require urgent action. There is no time for complacency: like all the other fundamental questions of justice raised by *Populorum Progressio* it is a test of our ability to act in solidarity with each other as human beings. Another critical issue not explicitly raised in the document, but rightly raised in this book, is the issue of gender. We must not forget that gender is itself a risk factor threatening human security and the right to participate in society: the secret violence of household abuse, the private oppressions of lack of property or inheritance rights, the lifelong deprivations that go with lack of schooling and the structural problem of political exclusion. Women are particularly at risk from a resurgence of fundamentalisms, of whatever faith. In order to tackle this threat, I believe it is necessary for faith adherents to place the empowerment of women at the centre of their own strategic thinking. Women must be enabled to participate fully and equally in decision-making within the faiths themselves and their concerns need to be embraced as priorities in prayer, advocacy and activism.

What I began to appreciate as President of Ireland – on visits, for example, to Somalia and Rwanda – and became convinced of during my five years in the UN, is that the underlying causes of practically all human insecurity are an absence of a capacity to influence change at personal or community level, exclusion from voting or participating in any way in national decision-making, and economic or social marginalisation. The key to change lies in empowering people to secure their own lives. For this they need the means to try to hold their governments accountable, at local and national levels.

This is why the communities of rights activists and of development specialists can learn a great deal from each other. The vision set out in *Populorum Progressio* has been translated in part into the political commitment of the Millennium Development Goals, which were developed from a UN summit in 2000. They call for only the most basic elements for survival by 2015: that hunger be halved, poverty reduced, and health and education made more widely available. As we seek to realise these rather limited aims, however, we must think in terms of the full range of claimable rights that we all possess.

The indications are that some of the Millennium Development Goals will not be met, particularly in sub-Saharan Africa, on the basis of progress made so far. Whether – and how – we reach these aspirations is a challenge for us all, and a test of whether we have really heard the call to justice boldly made by *Populorum Progressio* 40 years ago.

Activists in the Catholic tradition will, I am sure, find the articles in this book inspiring and helpful in deepening their vision and commitment to an ethical shaping of globalisation. I take this opportunity to commend the work of so many Catholic individuals and organisations working for a more just world where the dignity of all human beings is respected. Perhaps others, curious about the passion and endurance of these efforts, will also draw some inspiration and vision from the articles contained in this book. I would like to wish the International Jesuit Network for Development every success in the publication of this volume.

Mary Robinson
New York, February 2007

Why the Message of Populorum Progressio is Still Needed Today

Justin Kilcullen

The world of the new millennium is in a state of flux: political, economic and social realities have changed radically since the collapse of communism in the early 1990s. For an organisation like Trócaire, the Irish Catholic development agency, such changes pose a real challenge. How can we ensure that our work remains relevant to the reality of the world we live in and that we are addressing the real and vital issues that impact on the lives of the world's poorest people? Recently, we have completed a thorough examination of our work in order to address these issues and to set out our path for the coming ten years.

As part of this re-examination, we went back to our foundation document, the pastoral letter entitled *Bishops of Ireland on Development*, published in 1973, six years after *Populorum Progressio*. The pastoral takes up just two sides of an A4 sheet. This was the message of the encyclical distilled for popular consumption. It was a call to action, responding to Pope Paul's plea towards the end of his encyclical:

> ... how crucial is the present moment, how urgent the work to be done. ... At stake are the survival of so many innocent children ... at stake are the peace of the world and the future of civilisation. It is time for all men and all peoples to face up to their responsibilities. (n. 80)

The mandate for Trócaire outlined in the pastoral letter drew heavily on *Populorum Progressio*. The political and economic analysis in both documents is very similar. The issues of the day are all there – growing poverty and inequality in the world, the fact that we are rich partly because others are poor, a need for increased aid, the responsibility to establish fair trading relationships, our duties as Christians in justice towards poor peoples and countries.

14

These are all issues which Trócaire continues to deal with today. But what of the many issues that emerged in the intervening 40 years: the role of women in development, the globalised economy, the environmental crisis, the HIV pandemic? Pope Paul could not have foreseen all of these developments. Nonetheless, what he has left us in his teaching are the principles of reflection and criteria of judgement with which we can continue to analyse the present reality. We can continue to apply the teaching of the encyclical as we plan our responses to the modern world. In this way, *Populorum Progressio* is a living document – it is not frozen in its own historical reality. At the same time, it affirms the relevance of the church's teaching, a relevance that remains because it is always linked to the gospel of Christ.

Some Key Messages of Populorum Progressio
What are some of the key messages of *Populorum Progressio* and what is their relevance today? They might be summarised as follows:

- The need for a keen sense of urgency at the state of the world.
- The temptation to greed and the need for a global vision.
- Authentic human development and the universal purpose of created things.
- Development is the new name for Peace.

Need for a Sense of Urgency
Whether it is the plight of children in Africa, the plummeting life expectancy (now 46 years) on that continent due to HIV/AIDS, or the fact that almost one third of the world's population, 1.9 billion people, live on less than €1.60 per day, the urgent call for action for justice that Pope Paul makes in his encyclical is as necessary today as when it was written. While there have been many advances in different parts of the developing world, both the plight of Africa and the growing inequalities in Asia and Latin America that see hundreds of millions trapped in poverty, demand urgent radical reforms of the world's economic, social and financial structures. The scandal of poverty in a world of plenty is everywhere – the sense of hopelessness and fear in the Darfur camps for displaced persons, the

children scavenging on the rubbish tips of Central America, and the exploitative working conditions that so often underpin the western world's access to cheap toys and gems, clothes and fuel.

The situation in Africa is particularly worrying. The year in which *Populorum Progressio* was published, 1967, was a time of great optimism for that continent. Newly independent states had ambitious plans to educate their people, provide modern health services, and develop economically. Indeed, for quite some time steady progress was made. But war, the proxy wars of the old Cold War divide, and the failure of governance, set back the development process. Natural disasters have become more prevalent as climate change has begun to take effect. The debt crisis, already beginning to manifest itself in the 1960s, stifled all hopes of economic recovery. Now the HIV pandemic is both a symptom of this growing poverty and a contributing factor to it.

When heads of state and government of member states of the United Nations gathered in New York in 2000 to launch the Millennium Declaration, there was renewed hope that real progress would soon be made. The Millennium Development Goals (MDGs), derived from the overall objectives of the Declaration, set out clear targets against which the fight against world poverty could be measured. The first goal, that global poverty would be halved by the year 2015, set the context for the other major targets – progress to be made in health, education, food security and so on.

The governments of the developing countries undertook to put in place programmes to achieve these goals. The eighth MDG, termed 'a new partnership for development', is the goal that applies to the donor countries. To match the commitments of the poorer countries, the donor countries undertook to increase aid and to reform debt and trade structures in order to generate the necessary funds to achieve the goals. In addition, they undertook to streamline and coordinate the global aid effort to make it more effective and less burdensome on developing countries. Missing from MDG 8 – but clear in the other seven goals – are clear targets by which progress can be measured. As a result, progress has been mixed – to say the least. In implementing the

MDGs, we see little response to Pope Paul's demand for urgent action.

For example, where is the sense of urgency about creating more just trade relations? The Doha round of the WTO trade talks, heralded as the 'Development Round', representing a new deal for the world's poor, is now three years overdue with no resolution in sight. Rather than focus on the world's poor, as promised, the rich countries have kept a beady eye on each other, more anxious to maintain competitive advantage than to seek to deliver reforms to the benefit of the poor. On the need for just trading relations, Pope Paul posed the question:

> Who is there who does not see that such a common effort aimed at increased justice in business relations between peoples would bestow on developing nations positive assistance, the effects of which would be not only immediate but lasting? (n. 61)

Alas, the answer to that, presumably rhetorical, question is: 'An embarrassingly lengthy list of luminaries from the world of politics and economics!' Would Pope Paul have ever conceived that so logical a step to overcome poverty would have been frustrated for so long?

The global position on aid and debt relief is little better. The PR successes of the Make Poverty History campaign in 2005, and the earlier Jubilee Campaign for debt relief, were indeed significant. However, the promises made in the context of the Gleneagles G8 Summit in July 2005 to increase aid and debt relief are already looking somewhat threadbare. While the global figure for development aid reached a record US$106.8 million in 2005, most of the additional aid can be accounted for by aid to Afghanistan, Iraq, and to South East Asia in the wake of the December 2004 tsunami. Debt relief to Nigeria is also a key element in the increase. If this is deducted from the overall aid to sub-Saharan Africa, then aid to this, the poorest part of the world, fell in real terms by 2.1 per cent in 2005 – this, in the so-called 'year of Africa'!

Debt relief in general is doing little better. The Gleneagles agreement promised 100 per cent debt relief from multilateral creditors (for example, the International Monetary Fund (IMF) and the World Bank) to all developing countries. So far, there has been limited relief (from 21 to 79 per cent) for just 18 such countries. In effect, the debt crisis cannot be resolved without a fundamental change to the structures of international finance and radical changes to the criteria set down for debt relief, which must put human development, and not harsh economic calculations, at the heart of the debt relief agenda.

On all these issues – trade, aid and debt – there is clearly still not the political will to implement the effective and far-reaching reforms that are required to tackle global poverty and achieve the MDGs. For the poorest countries, the result of this lack of political will is that, at the current rate of progress, the MDGs are behind schedule by over one hundred years!

The Temptation to Greed and the Need for a Global Vision

The major scandal of the today's globalised world is the growing inequality that characterises it. It is of little comfort on rereading *Populorum Progressio* to note that Pope Paul had warned of such an outcome of uneven economic growth. The modern world now stands condemned by Pope Paul's analysis of such selfish activity: 'Both for nations and for individuals avarice is the most evident form of moral underdevelopment' (n. 19).

The following facts highlight the extent of global inequalities:
- In 2005, the wealth of the richest 20 people in the world amounted to $430 billion. This is more than the total income of 719 million people living in sub-Saharan Africa.
- The cost of meeting the Millennium Development Goals, an estimated $50 billion, is roughly equal to only 0.2% of global income.
- Europeans and Americans spend over $1 billion a month on pet food while 852 million of the world's people experience chronic hunger.
- Europeans spend $1 billion a week on cosmetics and toiletries while nearly 3 billion people lack access to basic sanitation.

These statistics point to a growing gap between those who are able to grasp the benefits of globalisation and those who have been left behind. Yet the numbers do not reveal fully the human cost of such inequality. Behind each statistic lies a real person. Their cares and dreams as mothers and fathers, friends and children are not so distant from our own. They, too, strive for a safe home and clean environment, a secure income to provide for their family, a healthy and long life and a better future for their children. Yet they have meagre incomes and no safety net to keep them going in times of need. They often face chronic and terminal illness and have little access to hospitals or medicines. Many have had to flee their homes due to armed conflict or natural disasters. The daily experience of poverty is often felt in a lack of control over their own lives, a sense of powerlessness, injustice, exclusion and denial of their rights.

Such poverty has become part and parcel of the process of globalisation which drives modern economic development. On the one hand, there are those who through geographical location, privilege or hard work can grasp the opportunities offered by the market-based global economy. On the other hand, there is the majority who, as a result of unjust social and economic structures, cannot avail of these benefits. But what do those same unjust social and economic structures say about the so-called developed world? As Pope Paul asks us, can there be authentic human development without morals? The rampant consumerism of today's developed world condemns us, as Pope Paul had warned, to being morally underdeveloped.

The lack of urgency, the self-centred nature of modern development, can only be overcome by creating a new global vision of how a just world might be achieved. The Millennium Development Goals have pointed in the right direction, but certainly lack ambition. Why only a halving of world poverty? Where is the leadership and the political will necessary to achieve these Goals to come from? Has the time again come for the Church to bring to the world a new and challenging vision of the future, particularly in the context of the growing environmental crisis, perhaps the greatest manifestation of the greed of the wealthy countries?

Authentic Development
and the Universal Purpose of Created Things

In the late 1990s, a colleague from another Catholic development agency told this story at a meeting discussing the impact of
the IMF structural adjustment programmes (SAPs) on Zambia.
Driving through a rural area on a research project in relation to
SAPs, she encountered the following scene: a man in a field
pushing a plough to which three children were shackled. For
me, this image illustrates so clearly the moral bankruptcy of the
fiscal policies that the indebted countries were compelled by the
IMF to follow during the 1970s, 1980s and 1990s. Children had
been reduced to the level of draft animals in a country that could
no longer provide basic education or health services to its population, nor guarantee basic levels of food supply. Under structural
adjustment, the population was compelled to pay fees for all services, the economy was geared to export production to raise the
hard currency needed to repay the debt. Attendance at school
and clinics plummeted. The country went into a spiral of decline.

Pope Paul tells us: 'Development cannot be limited to mere
economic growth'; rather, 'to be authentic' it must promote the
good of every person and of the whole person (n. 14). He warns
of the imbalance of power between the rich and poor nations
and speaks of the dangers of 'increasing disproportion', the
need for contractual justice between nations, and for equity in
international agreements. Such principles were ignored in the
development of the international financial institutions and the
financial architecture that they created. More recently, there has
been a belated recognition, based on sore experience, of the need
for an approach focused more on human development rather
than simply economic growth. At the heart of this is recognition
that sustainable development requires the participation of communities and peoples in the development process, and that basic
human needs must take precedence in development planning.
There is also a growing recognition of the role of community.
Pope Paul speaks of communal responsibility and the reality of
human solidarity.

Complementing this principle, Pope Paul reasserts the teaching of the Second Vatican Council that: 'God intended the earth and all it contains for the use of all men and peoples, so created goods should flow fairly to all, regulated by justice and accompanied by charity' (n. 22). The reform, barely started, of international political and economic structures, including the structures that govern trade, is critical to attaining the conditions in which people can aspire to authentic human development and a fair share of the riches of this earth. If these two principles, as outlined in the encyclical, were to underpin the work of development into the future they would provide the necessary impetus to enable real progress towards the achievement of the Millennium Development Goals.

Development is the New Name for Peace

To employ a modern marketing phrase, the 'signature theme' of *Populorum Progressio* is undoubtedly 'development is the new name for peace'. Pope Paul asks: 'For, if the new name for peace is development, who would not wish to labour for it with all his powers?' (n. 87)

Earlier in the text, he writes:

> Peace cannot be limited to a mere absence of war, the result of an ever precarious balance of forces. No, peace is something that is built up day after day, in the pursuit of an order intended by God, which implies a more perfect form of justice among men. (n. 76)

In the 1990s one could set out to walk across Africa from Angola on the Atlantic coast to Eritrea on the Red Sea and never leave a war zone. Angola, Zaire, as it then was, Uganda, Southern Sudan, Ethiopia and Eritrea – it was just one enormous battlefield. At one point, there were nine African armies fighting in Zaire. Thankfully, most of these wars have come to an end or are greatly reduced in their intensity with peace agreements being negotiated. But in no way can we say that Africa is at peace. Whole populations have been uprooted, millions have died, even more injured and maimed. States are brittle, trying to rebuild themselves under some form of embryonic democracy.

At the beginning of his encyclical, Pope Paul refers to the establishment a short time before of the Pontifical Commission for Justice and Peace 'so as to further the progress of poorer peoples, to encourage social justice among nations, to offer less developed nations the means whereby they can further progress' (n. 5). The work of justice and peace is central to development today. The formation of individuals and communities to understand their rights, to demand their participation in the decisions that will shape their lives, and to hold their elected representatives to account is critical to the development process. From such work, authentic human development can ensue, resources can be put at the service of the population at large, corruption actively countered and mature political societies emerge. It will take at least a generation, probably longer, but such work is surely the only lasting hope for the poorest and war-stricken countries of the world. True peace, as Pope Paul says, is something that is built up day after day.

Agencies such as Trócaire collaborate in many countries with the Justice and Peace Commissions, from parish to national level. Such collaboration is a distinguishing feature of the work of the Catholic development agency, an aspect that enables our engagement with poor communities in a way that is beyond the many secular organisations working in the field. It marks real solidarity between the faithful of the rich and poor worlds, and begins to make real the principle stated in the encyclical: 'The peoples themselves have the prime responsibility to work for their own development' (n. 77).

Conclusion

We can conclude that the message of *Populorum Progressio* is indeed still needed today. Yet, a question lingers: 'Is the message of *Populorum Progressio* enough for today's world?' While the principles and criteria of judgement given to us by Pope Paul remain constant, there inevitably comes a time when a new elaboration of those same principles and criteria in the modern context is required. It is interesting that Pope John Paul II (1987) thought it appropriate to publish an encyclical *Sollicitudo Rei Socialis* (*The Social Concern of the Church*) on the twentieth anniversary of *Populorum Progressio*. That encyclical, written before the fall of communism in Eastern Europe, laid emphasis on human rights, solidarity, the structures of sin, and addressed the ecological concerns of the time. The 20 years since then have seen enormous changes following the fall of the Berlin Wall: the growth of globalisation, the emergence of a new form of warfare following the atrocities of 9/11, and, increasingly, the environmental crisis.

The encyclical, *Deus Caritas Est*, issued by Pope Benedict XVI (2006), was widely welcomed for its reflections on the nature of love, and how this love manifests itself in the work of charity. A question remains though – is *Deus Caritas Est* part of the body of the social teaching of the church? I am inclined to think not. It is quite different in character to the social encyclicals, which are addressed to the wider world. *Deus Caritas Est* is more a reflection than a call for action. It seeks to deepen Christian understanding of the meaning of charity in the 21st century.

In a vastly changed world perhaps it is time for a restatement of the urgent need for action. The context this time is surely the ever-worsening environmental crisis. Perhaps there is no greater manifestation of the inequalities of today's world than that the poorest people and poorest countries will carry the burden, in the form of environmental disasters including water and food shortages, of the squandering of the earth's resources by the wealthy countries. It is not that poor people will just remain chronically poor in a world of plenty, but that what little they have will be destroyed by our overdevelopment and greed.

Pope Paul began his encyclical with the words: 'The development of peoples has the church's close attention ...'. It is surely time to give fresh expression to that close attention which is so constantly demanded.

References

Pope Benedict XVI (2006) *Deus Caritas Est* (*God is Love*), Encyclical Letter, 25 December 2005, London: Catholic Truth Society.

Pope John Paul II (1987) *Sollicitudo Rei Socialis* (*The Social Concern of the Church*), Encyclical Letter, 30 December 1987, London: Catholic Truth Society.

Populorum Progressio:
Sowing the Seeds for Liberation Theology

Jon Sobrino SJ

I am not a specialist in the church's social teaching, and I am not going to analyse *Populorum Progressio* in detail. Other contributors to this book will more than adequately do this. In this article I would like to offer two reflections on, firstly, particular issues that have been important to me over the 40-year period since the encyclical was published, and which remain relevant today, and, secondly, on some contemporary problems that we need to explore. What is at stake here is the salvation and humanisation of a civilisation that is gravely ill.

Global reality

Populorum Progressio argues a fundamental point that one must never take for granted: the fact that our existence is global. The encyclical begins, 'Today it is most important for people to understand and appreciate that the social question ties all men together, in every part of the world' (*Populorum Progressio*, n. 3). Human beings, whether they know it or not, whether they like it or not, exist in relationships not only with their families, their localities, their countries, their churches, but with more than six billion other human beings, and yet there is almost no awareness of this fact, which ought to be a fundamental given in our knowledge, our actions and in our hopes. Furthermore, in a world that is so proud of having achieved globalisation, there is a network of relationships within the world that is quite unknown. There is a conspiracy of silence about humanity as it is. Consciously or not, we are abusing an immense number of human beings. They have no name, no history. They do not exist.

If we accept this reality of global existence, at least in theory, the question arises whether we think of ourselves as a species or as a family. Here something fundamental is at stake. Once we get beyond empty and hypocritical words, we in the world of abundance do not understand ourselves as part of a human family. Matters are made worse when human beings are understood through Darwinian theory, where only the fittest survive. Worse still, if those who survive live very comfortably, possessing all they need and holding the balance of power, understand their fate as a manifestation of destiny. This, however, is the unconscious reality of the first world.

Oppressors and Oppressed

It is in this context that we have to reflect on a quotation from the encyclical: 'The hungry nations of the world cry out to the peoples blessed with abundance' (n. 3). Such a cruel reality has to be condemned; this is quite essential if we are to be true to the biblical prophetic tradition, to the message of Jesus, to the letter of James, to the life of Archbishop Romero, and to liberation theology. The simple contrast of hunger and opulence is something to be denounced, as we find in the parable of Dives and Lazarus, and in the Lucan beatitudes and curses. This denunciation comes to us from the oppressed of today and always, the starving people – a reality that is all too present as something we can see, hear, touch and smell. The rich world marginalises these people, however, and situates them in a mental hinterland and it is there too we situate God, so that he cannot bother us much.

The harsh language of condemnation is no longer fashionable. Yet John Paul II used strong words. In 2003, he spoke of 'the war of the powerful against the poor' (*Pastorem Gregis*, n. 67). While in Canada in 1984, he solemnly declared that: 'poor people and poor nations, poor in different ways, not only lacking in food, but also deprived of freedom and human rights, will sit in judgement on those who take these goods away from them'.[1] In general, however, people do not talk like this now. Instead they try to bury the cruel conflicts of today's world, speaking glibly, naïvely or hypocritically of 'globalisation', as if the conditions in this world were the same for everyone or at least becoming that way. The reality is, however, that since the fall of the Berlin wall, we are living within an all-embracing empire where radical differences exist.

From a Christian perspective, it is absolutely necessary that we call to mind the scandal in the very existence of poverty alongside great riches, and of the oppression that the rich exert on the poor. By doing so, we call to mind a central category in our faith that is now also very much in oblivion: *sin*. This idea is not very common in a 'doctrine' that aims to address everyone and something that is offered to us as fundamentally rational, not as something essentially religious, but when the idea of sin disappears, something fundamental disappears: sin is that which deals death, that which caused the death of the Son of God, that which continues to deal death to the daughters and sons of God. The existence of sin in the world becomes very clear when we see the 'crucified people' – to use a category central to the thoughts of Archbishop Romero and Ignacio Ellacuría. We are not used to looking at things in this way, however. We are more like the early *conquistadors*, accused by Friar Antonio de Montesinos in 1511 of being asleep to the plight of the native population.

Nor must we forget, as we focus above all on the world that produces it, that 'sin' is connected with 'conversion' – something always necessary, particularly today. Conversion is not simply a matter of bringing about a few changes, however welcome these changes may be or however positively directed. Conversion rather, is a matter of a different, even contradictory, way of being and acting. To use Ellacuría's language, we need to *revertir la historia* – re-orientate history.

If we come then to the church, it becomes clear that the church can only talk in its social teaching about sin and conversion if it has some credibility. As long as we are talking about 'doctrine', credibility is a matter of conceptual rationality and acute analysis – there is certainly no problem with this. When it comes to the church's 'praxis', however – educational, compassionate, prophetic and idealistic – credibility arises from the church's clear defence of the 'starving people' and the condemnation of the 'people in luxury'. The church's 'praxis' takes a risk by condemnation, but does so in a spirit of fortitude, which generates an inevitable sense of hope and of solidarity. A clear example of this was the social teaching of Archbishop Romero. The rationally expounded truth of his pastoral letters, and his firmness in the face of persecution, gave credibility to his 'social teaching'.

Integral Salvation

This idea of integral salvation has, since Vatican II, become sacred doctrine. In *Gaudium et Spes*, we read: 'For the human person deserves to be preserved; human society deserves to be renewed. Hence the focal point of our total presentation will be man himself, whole and entire, body and soul, heart and conscience, mind and will' (*Gaudium et Spes*, n. 3). *Populorum Progressio* reiterates this when it speaks of development. Development, it reminded us, requires technology, but, more importantly, it also needs a new humanism, which enables one to embrace the higher values of love, prayer, and so on. The encyclical continues: 'This is what will guarantee man's authentic development – his transition from less than human conditions to truly human ones' (n. 20).

We have to maintain the idea of a comprehensive humanisation. This is necessary and urgent because today's civilisation of wealth has not produced a more humane world, but rather a dehumanised one, as Ellacuría puts it. It is increasingly important for the church – the sacrament of salvation – to make explicit the different dimensions of salvation and perdition. The church needs to know just which salvation (with all the complexity this term involves and the historical content) it should be promoting as church teaching. It is therefore important to insist that salvation is *social, historical, personal* and *transcendent*, even if it is not always possible to distinguish these clearly. Moreover, salvation is simultaneously *a positive state of affairs*, and the process leading to that state. Finally, we need to remember something that is often forgotten: salvation in both these senses is dialectical, and at times conflictive. It occurs in opposition to other realities, and sometimes in the struggle against them.

If we are trying to be specific about the complexity of salvation, perhaps we can say the following.

(i) Salvation is life (the overcoming of basic deficiencies) as opposed to poverty, sickness, death. Salvation is dignity (respecting people and their rights) as opposed to neglect and disdain. Salvation is liberty as opposed to oppression.

27

(ii) Salvation is a relationship of sisters and brothers among the human family – a concept to be contrasted with the Darwinian understanding of humanity as simply a species.

(iii) Salvation is fresh air, that the spirit can breathe in order to move towards what makes for a fully human life (honesty, compassion, solidarity, openness to some form of transcendence) as opposed to what dehumanises (egoism, cruelty, individualism, arrogance, positivism).

We have to insist that salvation, as a process, occurs as something counteracting structures of oppression; hence salvation takes the form of liberation. Often it is not just that one has to struggle against the evils generated by structures; rather, one has also to attack the evil at its root. Hence salvation becomes redemption, where it has to address sin. It is part and parcel of redemption that the struggle with sin is not only from outside but also from within.

Structures, Dictatorship and Revolutionary Insurrection

For us, especially in Nicaragua and El Salvador, it was very important that *Populorum Progressio* broached these themes to which the bishops of Latin America returned at their 1968 Medellín Conference. Ours was, and is, a situation 'where there is manifest, longstanding tyranny which would do great damage to fundamental personal rights and dangerous harm to the common good of the country' (n. 31). In the Medellín Documents, in the chapter on 'peace', the bishops drew on *Populorum Progressio* and they made a statement that was both innovative and important: 'Revolutionary insurrection can be legitimate' (Medellín Conference Documents 1968, n. 19). Nevertheless, both the encyclical and the Medellín conference took into account all the harm that an insurrection can cause, and therefore encouraged nonviolent methods for the struggle against injustice, as did Archbishop Romero.

I am recalling this text because it sheds important light on the structural reality of sin, and its extreme seriousness – to the point of speaking of dictatorships not only vested in persons but also in structures. It also sheds light on what we have to do to counteract these dictatorships – to the point of seriously raising the question of revolutionary insurrection. Such an option might make sense in the face of very serious evils; the document considers it a temptation, because normally it leads to new imbalances and new damage. Indeed, it can become a greater evil than the one it seeks to combat. This in no way detracts, however, from the extreme seriousness of the problem with which we have to deal: an injustice crying to heaven; whole populations lacking what they need, living in a dependency that prevents them from taking any initiative or responsibility, or from enjoying any possibility of cultural development or participation in social and political life (see n. 30). The limitations of violent solutions must in no way be allowed to weaken people's costly, risky commitment to the struggle against injustice.

In their own time, Romero and Ellacuría drew on the texts of *Populorum Progressio* and Medellín in order to see when the struggle in the specific historical situations they were living through was not legitimate. They always insisted, even when legitimate, that the struggle had to be conducted in the most humane way possible, seeking to avoid all the negative by-products of a violent struggle. At the theoretical level, this led to a profound and enriching debate on the legitimate use of violence, and also on what Ellacuría called 'the redemption of violence'. As has been said, it was beyond debate that there needed to be a serious struggle against injustice.

That was the situation in Latin America back then, but the problem has persisted right up to today, albeit in other forms. There has been no great proliferation of military dictatorships, but there has been a growth in the economic injustice that leads to poverty and exclusion. It cannot be said that every form of 'overt and prolonged tyranny' (n. 31) has disappeared.

However, beyond any matters arising from specific contexts, for me the most important point at stake that needs to be brought to a logical conclusion, is the fact that Christian existence is *conflictive* – both at a personal level, and also at an ecclesial one (a point that we were rather less aware of). People these days tend just to assume that serious violence on the part of oligarchies, armies and governments is something of the past. However, this dangerously smoothes over the elements of real struggle involved in faith, the fact that faith draws us into conflicts and into risk-taking. The Psalmist is right to speak of justice and peace embracing each other as an eschatological ideal. However, this in no way detracts from the fact that throughout history we have with all our might, struggled against injustice.

Rather than an out-and-out quest for peace at any price, it is the spirit of *Populorum Progressio*, and indeed of Medellín, that we still need today. There are new forms of covert war that prevent direct aggression from ever surfacing, with massive consequences and collateral damage. We need to struggle against these energetically. The same can be said of the ever-new forms of economic warfare: the injustice of international trade, and the cruel and hidden ways in which it benefits products from very wealthy countries.

A Text 'With Spirit'

Ignacio Ellacuría develops the idea of being 'with spirit'. When he spoke of the beatitudes, he made a synthesis of people who are materially poor as described in Luke, and individuals poor in spirit, as it appears in Matthew, with the result that he spoke of the 'poor with spirit'. In another context he insisted that the University of Central America should be a university 'with spirit'. It was on this basis that he would speak of a university that had a Christian inspiration. This was not merely a pious gesture; rather it expressed an intuition about how 'reason' in a university could be made fruitful by Christian 'inspiration'. This was what he meant by a 'university with spirit'.

I think that this principle can be extended to cover other texts, including those of the church's social teaching. They have to exhibit solid analysis; they need to be reasoned, and grounded in a proper sense of the Bible, of theology, of pastoral care, of the social sciences. At the same time they must be filled with spirit. If their ideas are profound, far-reaching and radical, if, at key moments, their language provokes something, if they are somehow weighted with credibility, and arouse reactions, then you can say that a text has spirit, and I think that *Populorum Progressio* was, to a considerable extent, a 'text with spirit'.

Texts need to contain true concepts, but it is spirit that gives them life. If spirit is there, they can inspire conviction and hope, prophecies and ideals, an urgent sense of the need for conversation. Then too, they acquire an emotional power that enables the words of the gospel to resound, even if the language is different.

This seems to me important if the text is not to remain a mere concept – however necessary and good this is for teaching purposes and for theoretical investigation – but rather to be able to inspire pastoral praxis within history. If spirit is there, it will be more difficult for social teaching to be forgotten, or hijacked by those with economic, military and political power, as often happens.

Finally, the spirit of a text depends on its historical and social context. Vatican II and Medellín produced texts with spirit because in that context there was a hope and a desire for liberation. Archbishop Romero produced texts with spirit because there was persecution and martyrs. However, sometimes one also has to cherish the text for its own sake – and this is important, because these days there are not so many documents 'with spirit'.

The Reception of the Encyclical

At the theoretical level it is often said that a doctrinal statement of the church has to be received by the faithful; there needs to be a *receptio*. This has been established with regard to doctrinal texts, but the idea applies to texts of all kinds, including social teaching. *Receptio* can be understood in terms of whether or not the text's content is accepted; but I believe that we should broaden the idea so that it also refers to whether the text produces joy or sadness, a sense of being supported or a sense of being attacked.

If we are to deal properly with a theoretical text, there certainly has to be a serious discernment at the outset as regards its *a priori* validity, but above all, we have to look at what happens later, at the *a posteriori* reactions it provokes, and on what basis. When it comes to social teaching, it seems very important to me to note the reactions it provokes among the poor and oppressed majorities and among the rich oppressive minorities. If the poor applaud and the rich protest, this is a good sign. If it is the other way round, then it is not.

In our country, *Populorum Progressio* caused a commotion. Some called the document communist – a sign that the encyclical was on the right lines. Those who disseminated it were persecuted by the powerful. The poor, for their part, intuitively recognised what was most fundamental in the document, and were grateful for it. The text was on their side. It was good news. Today we need robust social teaching, because global society is seriously ill. The nature of this illness is captured in the following quotations from people who are level-headed and responsible.[2]

> There is more wealth on the earth, but also more injustice. Africa has been called 'the dungeon of the world', a continental Shoah. 2.5 billion people are living on our planet with less than 2 euros a day, and 25,000 people daily are dying of hunger, according to the Food and Agriculture Organisation. Desertification is threatening the life of 1.2 billion people in about a hundred countries. Emigrants are denied any sense of kinship, or a sense that the earth belongs to them. The USA constructs a 1,500 km wall against Latin America; and Europe at the south of Spain, raises a barrier against Africa. This is not just wicked; it is also deliberate – *says the famous Brazilian bishop, Pedro Casadáliga.*

> It is the reality of capitalism which is responsible for the ethically appalling structuring of the world economy and of global relations: this is shameful, irrational and absurd in a world that is becoming more interdependent, with unjust poverty amid unprecedented wealth – *Luis de Sebastián*[3] *(2005).*

> When future generations judge our era, they will call us inhuman and shameless barbarians because of our enormous insensitivity when faced with the suffering of our own sisters and brothers ... 'If there were sufficient humanity and compassion among human beings to reduce the 225 largest fortunes of the world by just 4%, there would be enough to give food, water, health and education to all humanity – *Leonardo Boff (2006).*

Degrading Humanity

If one thing is to be drawn from these quotations, it is that our world does not engender life for the masses; it dehumanises. Thus the church's social teaching deals not only with life and death in the world, but also with what humanises and what degrades. It is on this that I want to expand a little now. If today's world does not support life for all when it can, this alone renders it inhumane – but it is also the case that the noxious environment that gives rise to many ways of existing and acting is also dehumanising. In such an environment, it is difficult for the human spirit to breathe fresh air. Ellacuría was already denouncing this: the civilisation of wealth degrades humanity. In what follows, I shall name some important realities, which – quite apart from their violation of the commandments of God's law (don't steal, don't kill, don't lie) – deeply degrade humanity.

One thing that degrades humanity is the covering up of the truth and the proliferation of lies. The rich and the poor are desensitised in ways that are planned, or at least manipulated, by important mass media. Victims are deprived, in ways that are taken for granted, of their basic human rights. There is corruption, whether crude or subtle, in many circles of power. Again this is taken for granted as part of the unquestioned dogma of gain. The reverence paid to the present imperial figure of power with all its excesses has a dehumanising effect. Augustine used to speak of a great thieving empire – *'imperium mágnum latrocinium'*. It is degrading in the way we follow its directives so efficiently or at least fail to challenge them when this would risk the 'good life', the 'success' and the 'security' that the West regards as its definitive salvation.

Another shameful reality is the slowness with which poverty is being overcome, even though the rich congratulate themselves that this is happening. To halve the incidence of hunger at the present rate of progress will take 145 years, not the 2015 deadline agreed by 189 heads of government when they signed the Millennium Development Goals.

A further dehumanising reality is the way in which the language of globalisation has become an ideology. Certainly it sounds better than the language of capitalism; globalisation connotes a kind of pleasing roundedness and fairness, given that all points on the globe are equidistant from its centre. However, what is not being said clearly is that globalisation is, at best, ambiguous. It can be a world civilisation, or it can be a form of conquest, with winners and losers. When people use the word, they do not consider whether we are talking about one thing or the other.

Also degrading is the ostentatious display of abundance. The elite enjoy themselves through the leisure industries. In contrast to this ostentation, however, there is simply silence about the South. For example, in 2005 *Médecins sans Frontières* published a top 10 list of the humanitarian crises most neglected and forgotten by the international media in 2005. This highlighted that the media have taken for granted that there are many crises, and therefore focus only on the most grievous and shameful, the 'humanitarian ones'. They take it for granted that such crises are normally neglected, and just ask about the 'most neglected'. At the top of the list remains the crisis in Democratic Republic of the Congo where millions of people are living in a situation of extreme poverty and daily violence that has recently escalated. Nevertheless, this passes completely unnoticed by the rest of the world. This silence is a reality that faces the Third World.

Degrading too is our impotence in the face of all this – impotence not just in the face of fanatical terrorism, but also in the face of state terrorism perpetrated against all law and all reason, justified in terms of security, and occasionally baptised as a defence of democracy.

It is degrading, too, that we live in complete insensitivity to the cruelty of a world that exemplifies all too well the parable of Dives and Lazarus, in which there is not going to be any change '... even if someone rises from the dead' (Lk 16:31). Degrading too is the abuse not only of mother earth, but also of the poor indigenous human beings. In sum, it is egoism that degrades humanity: an egoism that is part of the social and structural environment and the air that the spirit breathes. It becomes a simple fact of life: historically, personally and socially.

Let us finally say, it is dehumanising for democracy to be maintained as something absolutely sacrosanct, without being evaluated properly or subjected to critical scrutiny. The criticism of democracy is an important task, one that is long-term and far-reaching. Regarding its most overt champion, the USA, Ignacio Ellacuría believes that the USA does not respect the will of the majority of humanity, nor the sovereignty of other nations, nor even the directives that come from the overwhelming majority represented in the United Nations, nor the verdicts that come from tribunals in The Hague. It is degrading to humanity that all this keeps on being forgotten, and that the Western world does not have it at the forefront of its consciousness.

When we analyse democracy, we must go to the root of the problem. If we do not do this, then our analysis will only increase the degradation. Ellacuría was not content merely to judge how the democracies went about their business. His concern was for a world order that strived for the common good, the necessary basis for establishing an inclusive and just society in solidarity with the least advantaged. Democracy is not, therefore, just a political issue, but equally a social and economic one. In other words, a social democracy promotes change where there are unjust conditions in which the masses live. It follows that democracy makes sense in theory and in practice only if it is grounded in the lived reality of the masses, the large sections of the population that are impoverished and excluded by the dominant groups.

This converges to some extent with the idea of the 'church of the poor': the poor are at the heart of the church, both as a source of inspiration and as a principle around which the church is structured. It is this, too, that has to be present if we are to speak rightly of democracy. We need to have a serious re-think if the concerns of the poor are not at the heart of democratic structures. To neglect to do so degrades humanity.

A further quotation, this time from Jean Ziegler, a United Nations official with responsibility for the right to food, illuminates this inhuman world: 'Every child who dies of hunger in today's world has been murdered.'[4] What he says recalls the story of Ivan Karamazov.[5] Ivan's indignation is not consoled by the thought that children killed by a pack of dogs at the order of a former army lieutenant can go to a place where they will become part of a universal harmony. In his condemnation Ivan decides to return his entrance ticket to this heaven. It is in such a world, however, that we are living.

On 6 November 1989, Ellacuría gave an address that turned out to be his last, and was thus an apt statement 10 days before his assassination:

> It is only in a spirit of idealism and hope that one can have the faith

> and courage to try with all the poor and oppressed of the world to re-orientate history, to subvert it, and launch it in another direction … what on another occasion I have called co-pro-historic analysis – the study of the 'dregs' of our civilisation – seems to show that this civilisation is seriously ill, and that if we are to prevent it falling apart in disastrous and mortal fashion, we need to try to change it from within itself.

In my opinion, this is what today's world needs if it is to get beyond the cruelty and misery of subhuman existence. To obtain this, we need to add a principle that as far as I know, is not normally discussed in the social teaching of the church: *extra pauperes nulla salus*, 'there is no salvation apart from the poor'. This is something other than a specific proposal or a recipe for action. It represents, rather, an invitation to follow a path that is more humane, more of the gospel. Our hope is that it promises a salvation that the powers of this world cannot promise.

References
Boff, Leonardo (2006) 'Who Rules the World', *Witness Magazine*, 28 February 2006.

Notes
1. John Paul II, 1984. Speech made in Alberta, Canada. Quoted in Pawlikowski, J. T. 2004. 'John Paul II and the Vatican on the Global Market Economy' in *The Economy Project*, Oxford: G. K. Chesterton Centre for Faith and Culture.
2. Most of this second part has been developed in my article 'Extra pauperes nulla salus. Pequeño ensayo utópico-profético', *Revista Latinoamericana de Teología* 69.
3. Luis de Sebastián is a Professor of Economics at Escuela Superior de Administración de Empresas de Barcelona (ESADE). http://www.fespinal.com/espinal/llib/es135.pdf 'Problems of Globalisation', September 2005, Barcelona *Cristianisme i Justícia*. 2006. http://www.thewitness.org/article.php?id=1032.
4. Ziegler's comments were made on United Nations Radio, 5 October 2006. www.un.org/radio.
5. Ivan Karamazov is a character in Dostoevsky's *The Brothers Karamazov*. 'The Grand Inquisitor' was originally published as the fifth chapter of the fifth book of Dostoevsky's novel *The Brothers Karamazov*.

The Wrath of the Poor: Peace, Poverty, and Catholicism since Populorum Progressio

Mary Ann Cejka[1]

Among Catholic peace activists, one is likely to hear an occasional bemoaning that the Catholic Church, for all of its official pronouncements and widespread efforts for peace, is not known (nor is it at pains to be known) as a 'peace church' – not, at least, in the historical tradition of the Quakers, Mennonites, or Brethren. Catholics who labour for peace often suffer from the awareness that peace is central to the social teachings of their church, but other issues, both in the parishes and the public arena, mean that those teachings are, in the end, crowded out.

Just such a displacement of attention took place when *Humanae Vitae* (Pope Paul IV, 1968) was published sixteen months after *Populorum Progressio* (*On the Development of Peoples*, Pope Paul VI, 1967). Commentators on *Populorum Progressio* argue that the storm over *Humanae Vitae* eclipsed much potentially fruitful discussion of the encyclical, despite the fact that the former simultaneously engendered anger on Wall Street and a fertile flowering of sociotheological analysis in the Global South. While neither of these two encyclicals of Pope Paul VI was innocuous, time granted notoriety only to one – perhaps at the cost of the other.

History is replete with examples of demands for justice leading to violence before they lead to peace, if indeed they succeed in doing so – a fact that may explain some of the indignation with which conservatives received *Populorum Progressio*. The encyclical follows in the tradition of *Pacem in Terris* (Pope John XXIII, 1963), and the *Pastoral Constitution on the Church in the Modern World* (Second Vatican Council, 1965), by posing a direct connection between human development and peace – and correspondingly, between the failure of human development and conflict. As Drew Christiansen SJ pointed out in a 2001 workshop on

Catholic peacemaking at the United States Institute of Peace, the development which Pope Paul VI called for in *Populorum Progressio* is integral to the Catholic vision of peace, which consists of four elements: human rights, development, solidarity, and world order (Smock, 2001).

While an integral concept of human development is the focus of *Populorum Progressio*, all four elements of the Catholic vision of peace are present and interconnected throughout the encyclical. One must therefore proceed with caution in attempting to stay specifically on the scent of the peace theme in *Populorum Progressio*, and in summarising its treatment without diluting or oversimplifying it. A summary seems the most useful next step in a chapter such as this. It will be followed by a broad and necessarily general overview of the kinds of conflicts (and examples of them) that have taken place in the world since the publication of *Populorum Progressio*, and conclude with an equally broad analysis of the ways it has been heeded or not, and of the ways hindsight and history allow us to critique and perhaps even build upon its prophetic insights.

A Brief Summary of Teachings Related to Peace in *Populorum Progressio*

- Injustice creates the conditions for violence, and therefore the perpetrators of injustice bear some responsibility for violence that ensues due to the conditions they have created (nn. 8-9; n. 11).
- The desperate poverty of most of the world's people renders intolerable the excessive wealth of a minority of its people (n. 53).
- While violent responses to injustice are not encouraged (n. 31) violence can be averted in the first place by a more just allocation of goods among nations (n. 49).
- Both nationalism and racism present serious obstacles to the pursuit of justice and peace (nn. 62-63).
- Excess resources allocated for military purposes should be redirected toward development that will help to relieve poverty (n. 51).
- These are urgent tasks (n. 53; n. 55) for both nations and

individuals (n. 80), but particularly for government authorities (n. 84).

- To work against poverty by promoting economic, moral, and spiritual development is to advance the cause of peace (nn. 75-76).
- An effective world authority is necessary to bring all the world's nations together and promote their collaboration (n. 78).

The Cold War World of *Populorum Progressio*, 1957-1991

Populorum Progressio was published during a time of optimism over social, economic, scientific, and political advances taking place throughout the world. Many African nations had only recently cast off the shackles of colonial authority.[2] The older nations of the world regarded these developments with both hope and apprehension: Would the new nations thrive under independence?

Even as the era of colonialism drew to a close, the world had become a more dangerous place, partitioned between East and West along boundaries clearly delineated by the victors of World War II. The atomic bombing of Hiroshima and Nagasaki at the end of that war ushered in the nuclear age, during which the United States and the Soviet Union raced to devise, test, and stockpile ever more destructive weapons in ever greater numbers. Terms such as 'brinkmanship', 'deterrence', 'second strike capability', and 'mutually assured destruction' populated diplomatic discourse and political rhetoric, as both sides postured themselves to assure that a nuclear attack by one would result in the total devastation of both. Mutual animosity deepened in the early years of the 1960s with the building of the Berlin Wall, followed by the Cuban missile crisis – at which point the Cold War very nearly escalated into a nuclear war. Throughout the 1960s and continuing to varying degrees into the next two decades, the United States and the Soviet Bloc competed for worldwide dominance not only militarily but in the areas of science and technology (with an emphasis on space exploration) and industry, as well as ideology.

The gulf between East and West grew in depth and range as the

Cold War rivals eyed the developing countries of the South, now being referred to as the 'Third World'. There, they engaged in covert surveillance and proxy wars, devoting significant economic and military resources to expanding both their markets and their strategic interests. The Vietnam War, a tragedy born of colonialism but catastrophically intensified by East-West rivalry, began early in the 1960s and lasted until the middle of the following decade.

In the 20 years following *Populorum Progressio*, significant popular political movements arose. Some, particularly in Latin America, developed into guerrilla warfare. During this period, corrupt and/or dictatorial regimes, largely representing wealthy elites, held power in Argentina, Brazil, Chile, Bolivia, Peru, Colombia, El Salvador, Nicaragua, Guatemala, and Honduras. These regimes were opposed, in the latter seven countries, by armed revolutionary movements who championed, at least officially, the cause of the poor. But throughout the 1970s and 1980s, it was the poor who were slaughtered in droves – along with many priests, nuns, catechists, missionaries, and an archbishop.

By the early 1990s, as the Cold War ended, peace agreements were signed in a number of Latin American countries. Dictatorships had toppled in some. Except in Colombia – where the conflict drags on in a post-Cold War quagmire of stark inequality, drugs, racism, classism, and United States' intervention – refugees began to return to their homes. International attention was gradually diverted from Latin America by new crises erupting in the Balkans, Afghanistan, Timor,[3] and the Persian Gulf, where the emerging, post-Cold War, 'New World Order' was put to the test by an Iraqi invasion of Kuwait. The United States, which had approved $200 million in military aid to Iraq over the previous seven years,[4] led an international coalition in a United Nations-mandated mission to liberate Kuwait, citing, among other justifications, a need to prevent a subsequent Iraqi invasion of Saudi Arabia and the capture of its Hama oil fields. By the time American troops began to move out of the Persian Gulf in March 1991, Kuwait had been 'liberated'. Its oil fields, and those of Saudi Arabia, were saved from further threat of Iraqi encroachment, and the United States and its allies were likewise saved, for the time being, from an Iraqi monopoly on oil.

The 1990s: Genocide, 'Ethnic Cleansing' and Intra-national Conflict

By the mid-1990s, most of the 96 documented conflicts in the world were not between nations, but between factions within nations (Wallensteen and Sollenberg, 1996). Civil wars and intra-national conflicts were nothing new, but the conflicts of the nineties were not primarily over ideology or other Cold War issues (though some, like the war in the Balkans, were largely precipitated by the ending of the Cold War). Mostly, they were over land, control of resources, and identities – or some combination of these[5] – and brought on, in many cases, by the lingering poison of colonialism. For example:

- In the Philippines – long occupied by Spain (1565-1898) and the United States (1898-1946) – a conflict between Muslims and Christians on the southern island of Mindanao escalated into bombings, kidnappings, and burnings of mosques and churches, taking its place alongside a still-active Cold War conflict between the Marxist New People's Army (NPA) and the Philippine government.
- In Rwanda, once colonised by Germany (1896-1916) and Belgium (1916-1962), vicious ethnic hatreds erupted in a genocide that took the lives of an estimated one million Tutsi and moderate Hutu between April and July of 1994. The violence then spilled over, along with millions of refugees, into neighbouring countries.
- In Sri Lanka, ruled by Britain from 1796 to 1948, a long-standing conflict between the mostly Buddhist Sinhala majority and the mostly Hindu Tamil minority grew more complex and entrenched in 1990 when Indian peacekeeping forces withdrew in defeat, leaving the two opposing factions to engage each other in all-out war.
- In Sudan, a second civil war of the twentieth century had pitted northern, largely Arab people against southern, black Africans since 1983.[6] In the midst of this conflict, a 1991 power struggle among the southern elite began a

brutal, interfactional struggle that set black African peoples of south Sudan against one another.

Even as these conflicts found resolution or dragged on, as the case may be, a different sort of global threat was increasing in frequency and commanding headlines: 'public acts of destruction, committed without a clear military objective, that arouse a widespread sense of fear' (Juergensmeyer, 2003) – also known as *terrorism*.[7]

2001 to the Present: An Age of Terror

Terrorism is not a new phenomenon. It did not begin on 11 September 2001, nor has it been confined to attacks against or within the United States. The 1990s saw car bombings in New Delhi, subway bombings in Paris, truck and bus bombings in London, and nerve gas released in a Tokyo subway. In the United States, the World Trade Center was attacked for the first time in 1993, followed by the Oklahoma City bombing in 1995, and the 1996 bomb blast at the Olympics in Atlanta. United States embassies were attacked in Peru, Kenya, and Tanzania. In the Middle East, suicide bombings occurred regularly.

Only with the attacks of 11 September 2001 – in which members of the extreme Islamist group Al Qaeda hijacked passenger jets, flying two of them into the Twin Towers of the World Trade Center, one into the Pentagon, and a fourth, thanks to the heroic intervention of its passengers, into a Pennsylvania field – came the widespread, public awareness that a different sort of enemy employing a different type of strategy now posed a major threat to global security.

But the United States responded with a 'War on Terror', thus framing the problem along conventional lines of 'war' and, despite the abstraction and emotional appeal of defining 'terror' as its target, responded with methods more applicable to a localised, geographically identifiable enemy (such as a nation state). Less than a month after 11 September, United States and British forces began aerial bombardment of Afghanistan for the stated purpose of targeting Al Qaeda members and Afghanistan's Taliban[8] government, which had harboured them. In March of 2003, the United States and Great Britain, despite overwhelming international opposition, declared war on Iraq on the now dis-credited grounds that Iraqi leader Saddam Hussein had been in league with Al Qaeda and was preparing to use weapons of mass destruction against his enemies. At the time of writing, as many as 654,965 Iraqis (or 2.5 per cent of the Iraqi population) have died violent, war-related deaths since the beginning of the war (Burnham *et al.,* 2006).

The Cold War ended with the collapse of the Soviet Union, but nuclear weapons continue to proliferate. Eight states are known to possess them, and many others have nuclear reactors. During the week of this writing, the ominous news broke that North Korea – still separated from the South and isolated from the rest of the world, a tragic and volatile legacy of the Cold War – has tested a nuclear weapon. As these weapons proliferate, they are more likely to end up in the hands of extremist, non-state entities.

Genocide is a current reality in the Darfur area of Sudan, where an estimated 200,000 people died over a 31-month period (Burnham *et al.,* 2006). Many in Colombia, Sri Lanka, Democratic Republic of the Congo, Nepal, the southern Philippines, and much of the Middle East still live in constant fear of being bombed, shot, tortured, disappeared, or routed from their homes – whether by government-sanctioned military forces, paramilitaries, or 'terrorist' groups. The world's refugees, asy-lum seekers, and internally displaced persons currently number 20.8 million.[9] Amnesty International's 2005 Annual Report ob-served that during the previous year, 'the human rights of ordi-nary men, women and children were disregarded or grossly abused in every corner of the globe'.[10]

The Development of Peoples ... Toward Peace?

At this point – in history, as well as in this article – it seems ap-propriate to return to the teachings of *Populorum Progressio* on peace, braving its judgement on the course of the world – and the church – in the last 40 years. This is also an opportunity to as-sess, with the benefit of hindsight, the encyclical's limitations – not for the sake of dismissing it, but to understand better how its spirit may be lived and its teachings implemented, given the lessons of the past 40 years and the realities that confront us early in the twenty-first century.

The Poverty and Violence Connection

Following the attacks of 11 September 2001, an understandable reaction among many in the United States was to ask: 'Why?' – and more specifically, 'Why do they [the attackers] hate us?' It quickly became clear that only one answer, that proffered by the Bush administration, was officially acceptable: 'They' were 'evil-doers' who 'hate freedom' – meaning that we, in contrast, are freedom-loving doers of good, who were attacked unjustly due to the sheer evil of our attackers. This simplistic conclusion left little room for difficult questions about how others perceive America's disproportionate consumption of the world's re-sources; about its exploitative economic policies or history of self-serving military interventions abroad; about the silent com-plicity of the millions who benefit from these practices; or about what the Twin Towers may have symbolised to the half of the world's population living on less than two dollars a day.[11] Any such questions were met with outrage. The leaders and citizens of a wealthy and powerful nation appeared oblivious to the con-nection between their country's behaviour and the reactions it provokes elsewhere in the world.

Forty years ago, even before the Twin Towers loomed over it,[12] Wall Street had given *Populorum Progressio* an angry reception. The encyclical suggested that when people amass wealth as a re-sult of unjust practices, they invite violence: 'Continuing avarice on the part of [prospering peoples] will arouse the judgment of God and the wrath of the poor, with consequences no one can foresee' (n. 49). Today, it is no easier than it was then for the wealthy to face this fact. Today, however, it is also known that the poverty and violence connection is not as simple as *Populorum Progressio* made it seem. Not only have 40 years passed since the encyclical was written; 40 years of research in the social sciences – too voluminous to reference here in detail – have yielded fertile results, shedding light on a multitude of fac-tors that can fuel a conflict or quell it. Phenomena that might have been intuitively grasped before are now understood in their considerable complexity and with empirical certitude: for example, disappointed or frustrated expectations are more likely to lead to aggressive reactions than simple perceptions of injustice (Berkowitz, 1989; Grant and Brown, 1995; Kulik and Brown, 1979); the human tendency to comply in even minimally coercive situations – not limited to specific nations or personality types or criminals or terrorists – is distressingly easy to exploit in carrying out both unjust and violent agendas (Miller, Collins and Brief, 1995); people who work for peace may hold images of the divine and beliefs about justice in the world that are different from those who do not work for peace (Cejka, 2003). Not every 'underdeveloped' country is at war, not every victim of injustice turns to violence, and peace is sometimes achieved despite widespread poverty. Pope Paul did include sections in *Populorum Progressio* on nationalism and racism as obstacles to justice and peace, but the cognitive mechanisms by which negative stereotypes or enemy images (manipulated by street gangs and governments alike) can escalate violence (Keen, 1986; Holt and Silverstein, 1989; Silverstein and Flamenbaum, 1989), are better understood now than they were in 1967. Such research findings generally go ignored or unutilised, but they are available to those who wish to consider them.

Populorum Progressio seems to allow for at least some instances where 'revolutionary uprising' (n. 31) may be justifiable or even necessary. However, it also cautions that violent means can 'engender new injustices, introduce new inequities, and bring new disasters' (n. 31).

When the encyclical was first released, the bishops of Latin America – a continent then engulfed in political violence – welcomed it with lively interest. Meeting in Medellín, Colombia, the year after the encyclical was issued, they reflected upon the political realities of Latin American countries, many of them entrenched in unjust and oppressive political structures. The epic documents issuing from the Medellín Conference identified 'liberation' as a more critical issue than 'development'.[13] Following the publication of *A Theology of Liberation* in 1973 by Gustavo Gutiérrez, the concept of the 'preferential option for the poor' was embraced by the church – even at its highest levels – in much of Latin America.

Deck (2005) argues that *Populorum Progressio* demonstrated Pope Paul's sensitivity, both to the injustices perpetrated against the world's poor, and the danger that many of them face in confronting those injustices:

> Speaking out about the most elementary rights means persecution and even instant death in many places of the world ... One might ask those who wish to propose confrontational models for political change, now with the benefit of hindsight, what benefits were obtained for the poor and powerless, what human development came about as a result of the years of conflict in Central America during the 1980s. The answer remains ambiguous. (p. 307)

A hopeful development at the time of writing, however, is that several Latin American countries have new governments whose stated objectives bear some similarity to the principles of human development put forth in *Populorum Progressio*.

According to Christiansen, 'Catholic peacemaking has come to recognise the importance of non-violence, and indeed to formally adopt non-violence in significant ways' (Smock, 2001, p. 4) in the years since the publication of *Populorum Progressio*, particularly during the pontificate of John Paul II. This has led to 'a downplaying of just-war analysis in Vatican pronouncements, though it still utilises the just-war criteria in criticisms of acts of war the Holy See regards as immoral' (Smock, 2001, p. 5).

Nationalism and Racism
Pope Paul's observations regarding nationalism and racism (nn. 62-63) were confirmed by the horrible episodes of ethnic cleansing and genocide that characterised the decade of the nineties. Nationalism continues to be used as an excuse for violations of civil and human rights. While racism, among other variables, continues to fuel conflicts in Darfur, Colombia, Sri Lanka, and the Middle East, strides have been made toward unmasking its evil and stripping it of power; most notably, South Africa's brutal system of racial apartheid was brought to an end in 1994.

Money for Arms versus Money for Development.
In 2005, the world spent over a trillion dollars on military spending in general,[14] with almost half of that spent by the United States.[15] Five relatively wealthy nations – the United States, United Kingdom, Russia, France, and Germany – manufacture most of the world's weapons; and two thirds of those weapons

are sold in Asia, Africa, Latin America, and the Middle East.[16] In *Populorum Progressio*, Pope Paul cited his explicit appeal to nations at the 1964 Eucharistic Congress in Bombay, that they 'set aside part of their military expenditures for a world fund to relieve the needs of impoverished peoples' (n. 51). To this writer's knowledge, no such fund was ever established. Instead, countries recently free from colonial rule began quickly to amass large debts (see the relevant chapters in this volume) on loans from banks or multilateral creditors such as the International Monetary Fund – ironically, to finance development projects that were supposed to help them out of poverty. Even more tragically, an estimated 20 per cent of the loan money was used to purchase arms.[17] In countries of the Global South, then ruled by dictators and neo-colonial governments, arms purchased with loan money were used in campaigns of repression against large segments of their populations.

An Effective 'World Authority'

With 191 member nations in its General Assembly and the stated aims of facilitating cooperation in international law, international security, economic development, and social equity, the United Nations (UN), more than any other international body, continues to exemplify Pope Paul's hope for 'a world authority capable of taking effective action on the juridical and political planes' (n. 78). Its impressive achievements since its inception in 1945 encompass many instances of making and maintaining peace; promoting democracy, development, and human rights; protecting the environment; and strengthening international law, to name only a few.

To say that the UN has been at the forefront of these endeavours is to acknowledge both its successes and failures. No other international organisation of its size and scope exists to attempt what it has attempted on the world's behalf. It has consequently achieved what nothing else could achieve, and made mistakes that nothing else could make – in both cases, providing the world with hard lessons it would not otherwise have learned. The UN – due to an arguably cumbersome bureaucracy and its share of internal scandals – has not always been the 'effective' international authority called for by *Populorum Progressio*. Its efficiency and utility have additionally been hampered by the failure of some member states to pay their dues. The most damaging example of this failure in recent years has been the United States, where nationalist and isolationist factions succeeded in lobbying Congress to refuse dues payments to the UN as a way to force UN compliance with US objectives.

Despite the limitations of the UN – but also because of its potential – the Catholic Church, according to Christiansen, 'has tended to be internationalist in its outlook, to support the United Nations system' (Smock, 2001, p. 5) during the past 40 years.

Catholic Peace Efforts

It is no exaggeration to state that every collective Catholic effort for peace since *Populorum Progressio* (and perhaps even before it) has embodied a commitment to integral human development. This may be a sweeping assertion, but it is also hard to deny; it characterises both large and small Catholic peace efforts from the highest levels of church governance, right down to the grassroots. Many examples exist of bishops' conferences and individual bishops who have articulated the Catholic vision of peace and development within their own countries. They have also served as dispute mediators and as advocates for workers, immigrants, and prisoners, understanding both their mediation and advocacy as integral components of their pastoral responsibility as peacemakers.

Catholic social agencies, like the 162 that make up the Caritas Internationalis confederation, have evolved over the years from providing mere 'relief' to disaster victims, to embracing the need for development, to acknowledging the need for confronting unjust systems, to focusing on the active pursuit of skills for dealing with conflict – each new development building upon those before. Many Catholic universities now offer peace studies programmes with curricula based upon Catholic social teaching, as well as volunteer opportunities for students to experience for themselves the integral connection between justice and peace in the living out of their Catholic faith. Decades before *Populorum Progressio*, the Catholic Worker movement (starting in the United States) and Pax Christi (starting in France) both had regarded work for social and economic justice as integral to their efforts for peace. So does the Sant' Egidio Community, founded in Rome in 1968, and so do lesser-known, grassroots Catholic peacemaking initiatives like Kitusara in Sri Lanka, Peace Advocates Zamboanga in the Philippines, and the Nevada Desert Experience in the United States.

Some such efforts have an ecumenical or interfaith dimension. For example, in response to escalating violence between Thai soldiers and alleged Islamic militants on Thailand's Malay peninsula, Maryknoll missioners sponsored an interfaith gathering in August 2004 that 'led to programs to help young people in juvenile detention, opened classrooms to give children more schooling and started a cooperative store in a village that had no shops and little job opportunity except rubber tapping' (Monahan, 2006). They thereby improved relationships and promoted a sharing of resources between the opposing factions.

A Peace Church?
Still, I flash back to those Catholic peace activist friends of mine – the ones with whom I opened this chapter. They are right. *Populorum Progressio* has had some impact, as has all of Catholic Social Teaching. However, its impact is nowhere near as vast as it could have been. Do the millions of Catholics worldwide understand that working for peace by working for justice is integral to their faith? Rwanda taunts us with its memory of Catholics committing genocide against Catholics. Latin America taunts us with its huge gaps between rich and poor, and with its history, even in recent times, of wealthy Catholic elites violently repressing masses of (largely Catholic) poor. Just as *Humanae Vitae* had the unintentional effect of diverting attention from *Populorum Progressio*, so has official Catholic teaching in matters of personal morality – or personal piety, or details of Catholic liturgy – overshadowed Catholic social teaching on poverty, development, justice, and peace. Chalk it up to bad catechesis, or historical circumstances, or even the sheer size of the institution with its millions of members, but the fact remains that one can be a Catholic in good standing and have contempt for the poor, consume ex-

travagantly, thwart efforts at confronting unjust economic practices, clamour for the death penalty, and enlist to fight in any war, be it just or unjust.

Also limiting the church's ability to advance its peace and justice agenda are problems internal to Catholicism but well publicised in the secular news media. The exclusion of women and married men from priestly ministry, the intolerant treatment of homosexuals, the repeated violation of theologians' academic freedom and, most damningly, the abuse of children by paedophiles among Catholic clergy, have affected the church's institutional health and therefore its ability to act effectively, while at the same time diminishing its influence and credibility as a moral voice.

But even if we Catholics were all angels operating within a perfectly just ecclesial system, ours would not be a 'peace church' in the sense of the historic peace churches, whose emphases (and in many instances, expertise) are on the valuable skill sets of conflict resolution and conflict transformation – in other words, responding to existing violent conflict in the hopes of ending it or limiting its damaging effects. Within the past decade or so, awareness has grown among Catholic peace practitioners and scholars alike that we have much to learn about effective methods specifically for halting violence – whether or not justice has yet been achieved for all parties. Documentation of and reflection upon the Catholic peacemaking experience[18] is on the rise, and much more is needed.

With this need acknowledged, however, it is also true that within Catholic social tradition, peace is much more than the absence of war, the avoidance of war, or the end of war. According to Christiansen, the Catholic vision of peace is 'the positive realisation of the dignity of the whole human family' (Smock, 2001, p. 4). Peace is not just 'made' out of conflict, but built, day by day – with the bricks of human dignity, development, solidarity, and world order. This is an urgent task, Pope Paul wrote in *Populorum Progressio*: 'The very life of needy nations, civil peace in the developing countries, and world peace itself are at stake … Every individual and every nation must face up to this issue …' (n. 55; n. 80). Some have. Most have not. But the task is more urgent than ever.

References

Berkowitz, Leonard (1989) 'The Frustration-Aggression Hypothesis: An Examination and Reformulation', *Psychological Bulletin*, 106:1, 59–73.

Burnham, Gilbert, Riyadh Lafta, Shannon Doocy and Les Roberts (2006) *Mortality After the 2003 Invasion of Iraq: A Cross-sectional Cluster Sample Survey*. Retrieved 12 October 2006 from the Johns Hopkins Bloomberg School of Public Health, online Public Health News Center. www.jhsph.edu/publichealthnews/press_releases/2006/burnham_ir aq_2006.html.

Cejka, Mary Ann (2003) 'God, Justice, Gender, and the Enemy: Issues in Grassroots Peacemaking', in Mary Ann Cejka and Thomas Bamat (eds) *Artisans of Peace: Grassroots Peacemaking among Christian Communities*, Maryknoll, NY: Orbis Books.

Cejka, Mary Ann and Thomas Bamat (eds) (2003) *Artisans of Peace: Grassroots Peacemaking among Christian Communities*, Maryknoll, NY: Orbis Books.

Deck, Allan Figueroa (2004) 'Populorum Progressio', in Kenneth R. Himes, OFM (ed) *Modern Catholic Social Teaching: Commentaries and Interpretations*, Washington, DC: Georgetown University Press.

Grant, Peter R. and Rupert Brown (1995) 'From Ethnocentrism to Collective Protest: Responses to Relative Deprivation and Threats to Social Identity', *Social Psychology Quarterly*, 58:3, 195-211.

Gutiérrez, Gustavo (1973) *A Theology of Liberation: History, Politics, and Salvation*, Maryknoll, NY: Orbis Books.

Holt, Robert R. and Brett Silverstein (1989) 'On the Psychology of Enemy Images: Introduction and Overview', *Journal of Social Issues*, 45:2, 1-11.

Juergensmeyer, Mark (2003) *Terror in the Mind of God: The Global Rise of Religious Violence*, Berkeley, CA: University of California Press.

Keen, Sam (1986) *Faces of the Enemy: Reflections of the Hostile Imagination*, New York: Harper & Row.

Kulik, James A. and Rupert Brown (1979) 'Frustration, Attribution of Blame, and Aggression', *Journal of Experimental Social Psychology*, 15, 183-194.

Miller, Arthur G., Barry E. Collins and Diana E. Brief (1995) 'Perspectives on Obedience to Authority: The Legacy of the Milgram Experiments', *Journal of Social Issues*, 51: 3 (entire issue).

Monahan, L. (2006) 'Maryknoll in the Land of Buddha', *Maryknoll*, 100, 19-22.

Silverstein, Brett and Catherine Flamenbaum (1989) 'Biases in the Perception and Cognition of the Actions of Enemies', *Journal of Social Issues*, 45:2, 51-72.

Smock, David (2001) *Catholic Contributions to International Peace*, Washington, DC: United States Institute of Peace (Special Report, 69).

United Nations High Commissioner for Refugees (2004) 'Cartagena 20 Years Later', *Refugees*, 4, 22–31.

Wallensteen, Peter and Margareta Sollenberg (1996) 'The End of International War? Armed Conflict 1989–1995', *Journal of Peace Research*, 33:3, 353-370.

Church Documents

Conference of Latin American Bishops (CELAM) (1968) *Medellín Documents*, 6 September 1968.

Pope John XXIII (1963) *Pacem in Terris* (On Establishing Universal Peace in Truth, Justice, Charity, and Liberty), 11 April 1963.

Pope Paul VI (1968) *Humanae Vitae* (On the Regulation of Birth), 25 July 1968.

Pope Paul VI (1967) *Populorum Progressio* (On the Development of Peoples), 26 March 1967.

Pope Paul VI (1964) Special message to the world, delivered to newsmen during India visit, 4 December 1964; *Acta Apostolicae Sedis* 57 (1965), 135 (cf. *The Pope Speaks*, X, 275ff.)

Second Vatican Council (1965) *Pastoral Constitution on the Church in the Modern World*, 7 December 1965.

Notes

1. The author wishes to thank Thomas Bamat, James Kofski, William D. McCarthy, Tim O'Connell, and Ronald Pagnucco for their many valuable comments on a draft of this chapter.
2. Libya, Tunisia, and Ghana gained their independence in the 1950s, followed in the early sixties by Nigeria, Sierra Leone, Algeria, Congo, Kenya, and Tanzania (a merger of Tanganyika and Zanzibar).
3. See UNHCR, 2004.
4. See 'Arms Sales to Iraq 1973–1990,' Stockholm International Peace Research Institute. Retrieved 24 October 2006, from www.answers.com/topic/arms-sales-to-iraq-1973-1990.
5. As with Northern Ireland, South Africa and the Middle East, there were some conflicts that preceded the 1990s that were less directly related to the Cold War.
6. This conflict was also characterised by some residual Cold War ideology: the Marxist-Leninist Sudan People's Liberation Army dominated southern resistance efforts from the early eighties onwards.
7. Juergensmeyer (2003) points out that 'whether or not one uses "terrorist" to describe violent acts depends on whether one thinks that the acts are warranted ... If the world is thought to be at war, violent acts may be regarded as legitimate. They may be seen as preemptive strikes, as defensive tactics in an ongoing battle, or as symbols indicating to the

world that it is indeed in a state of grave and ultimate conflict.' Depending upon one's point of view, writes Juergensmeyer, the term 'militant' may be preferred to 'terrorist'.

8. The Taliban are a fundamentalist, Islamist militia that ruled most of Afghanistan from 1996 to 2001.

9. Retrieved 12 October 2006 from the web site of the United Nations High Commissioner for Refugees, Basic Facts section (www.unhcr. org/basics.html). Date of posting, 12 October 2006.

10. Retrieved 12 October 2006, from the web site of Amnesty International, 'Amnesty International Report 2005' (http://web. amnesty.org/report2005/index-eng).

11. Retrieved 17 October 2006, from www.channel4.com/ money/chat_vote_win/richometer/who_ww.html.

12. Construction of the Twin Towers began in 1966, the year before the publication of *Populorum Progressio*, and was completed in 1972.

13. In the years that followed, it became clear that 'development' as a positive or even salvific concept – especially when referring to economic, industrial, or technological development – had its limitations. Many proponents of such growth have been sanguinely oblivious to the environmental threats it might pose to the natural world. Moreover, the word often carries with it paternalistic and neocolonial overtones.

14. See table titled 'World and Regional Military Expenditure Estimates 1988–2005', Stockholm International Peace Research Institute. Retrieved 25 October 2006, from www.sipri.org/contents/ milap/milex/mex_wnr_table.html.

15. See table titled 'The 15 Major Spending Countries in 2005,' Stockholm International Peace Research Institute. Retrieved 25 October 2006, from www.sipri.org/contents/milap/milex/ mex_data_index. html.

16. See Desmond Tutu, 'Arms Trade is a New Slave Trade'. Retrieved 15 October 2006 from Ekklesia web site (www.ekklesia.co.uk/content/news_syndication/article_06103arms.shtml). Date of posting 10 March 2006.

17. See Patricia Adams, Odious Debts (www.threegorgesprobe. org/probeint/OdiousDebts/OdiousDebts/chapter12.html). Retrieved 15 October 2006.

18. For a recent international study and analysis of grassroots Catholic peacemaking efforts, see Cejka and Bamat (2003).

Peace and Development in Africa

Muhigirwa Rusembuka Ferdinand SJ

All of you who have heard the appeal of suffering peoples, all of you who are working to answer their cries, you are the apostles of a development which is good and genuine, which is not wealth that is self-centred and sought for its own sake, but rather an economy which is put at the service of human being. (*Populorum Progressio*, n. 86)

To celebrate the 40th anniversary of Paul VI's encyclical *Populorum Progressio* is not only an opportunity to revisit its past but also to scrutinise the signs of our times in Africa. It is within this context that we are reflecting on the theme of peace and development in Africa. Peace and development are intrinsically linked. On one hand, peace is a prerequisite, a condition *sine qua non*, of development. On the other hand, development includes peace as an order intended by God, as a form of justice among human beings.

In this chapter, I would like first to clarify the *status quaestionis* of peace and development in Africa; second to understand Paul VI's vision of development; and third to make explicit the interconnectedness of peace and development.

Status quaestionis
In contrast with other encyclicals, *Populorum Progressio* is not a scientific speech on how societies should be or on the way they should be constructed. Pope Paul VI begins his speech by what should be done because it is necessary to 'build a world where every human being, without discrimination of race, religion, nationality, can live plainly free of servitudes from other human beings and from a badly non-mastered nature; a world where freedom is not a simple word' (n. 47).

In the world today, when we scrutinise the signs of the times, 'the distance is growing that separates the progress of some and the stagnation, not to say the regression, of others' (n. 29). In fact, 'rich peoples enjoy rapid growth whereas the poor develop

54

slowly. The imbalance is on the increase: some produce a surplus of foodstuffs, others cruelly lack them' (n. 8). More than the imbalance between the industrially developed countries and developing countries, 'the world is sick. Its illness consists less in the unproductive monopolisation of resources by a small number of men than in the lack of brotherhood among individuals and peoples' (n. 66).

There is also 'the scandal of glaring inequalities' not merely in the enjoyment of possessions but even more in the exercise of power. 'While a small restricted group enjoys a refined civilisation in certain regions, the remainder of the population, poor and scattered, is deprived of nearly all possibility of personal initiative and of responsibility, and oftentimes even its living and working conditions are unworthy of the human person' (n. 10).

What is the situation in Africa? In *Ecclesia in Africa*, Pope John Paul II affirms that 'Africa, in spite of its great natural riches, remains in an economic situation of poverty. Nevertheless, it is gifted with a vast range of cultural values and of inestimable qualities which it can offer to the churches and to the whole of humanity ... Some of these cultural values, certainly, constitute a providential preparation for the transmission of the gospel; these values can bring about positive evolution of the dramatic situation of the continent, something which would facilitate the general recovery on which is based the development expected or hoped for each nation.'[1]

The present situation in Africa cannot be understood, however, without a correct understanding of its past, where colonisation has played a major role. Pope Paul VI affirms that 'colonising powers have often furthered their own interests, power or glory, and that their departure has sometimes left a precarious economy' (n. 7). However, one must recognise the important role played by the Catholic Church. Since the church's characteristic attribute is a global vision of man and of the human race, 'she has never failed to foster the human progress of the nations to which she brings faith in Christ. Her missionaries have built, not only churches, but also hostels and hospitals, schools and universities' (n. 12) in many African countries.

The situation in Africa is an intolerable scandal (n. 53) because peoples are striving to escape from hunger, misery, endemic diseases and ignorance (n. 1). In this context, development means 'freedom from misery, greater assurance of finding subsistence, health and fixed employment; an increased share of responsibility without oppression, insecurity, violence – in brief, to seek to do more, know more and have more in order to be more' (n. 6).

A Vision of Development

In *Populorum Progressio*, what is suggested about development is neither scientific knowledge nor technological know-how. It is a global vision of the human being, a perspective of human development. Paul VI states:

> development cannot be limited to mere economic growth. In order to be authentic, it must be complete: integral, that is, it has to promote the good of every human being and of the whole human being. As an eminent specialist (Jacques Lebret) has very rightly and emphatically declared: 'We do not believe in separating the economic from the human, nor development from the civilisations in which it exists. What we hold important is man, each man and each group of men, and we even include the whole of humanity'. (n. 14)

This vision of development will lead to 'the fullness of authentic development, a development which is for each and all the transition from less human conditions to those which are more human' (n. 20). By less human conditions, Paul VI means 'oppressive social structures, whether due to the abuses of ownership or to the abuses of power, to the exploitation of workers or to unjust transactions' (n. 21). Among the more human conditions he mentions: 'the passage from misery towards the possession of necessities, victory over social scourges, the growth of knowledge, the acquisition of culture, increased esteem for the dignity of others, the turning toward the spirit of poverty, cooperation for the common good, the will and desire for peace, the acknowledgment by men of supreme values, and of God their source and their finality' (n. 21).

Authentic development is not and cannot be reduced to simple economic growth. It embraces all aspects of peoples' life. It brings to the peoples who benefit from it the means of self-betterment and spiritual growth. There can be no progress towards the authentic development of human beings without the simultaneous development of all humanity in the spirit of solidarity, mutual support and accountability. Thus human fulfilment constitutes, as it were, a challenge and an ideal (objective). 'But there is much more: this harmonious enrichment of nature by personal and responsible effort is ordered to a further perfection. By reason of his union with Christ, the source of life, man attains to new fulfilment of himself, to a transcendent humanism which gives him his greatest possible perfection: this is the highest goal of personal development' (n.16).

At the Economic Level

In a global economy, 'unchecked liberalism' leads to 'the excessive inequalities of economic power' (n. 58), 'trade inequalities' (n. 56), 'economic dictatorship' (n. 59), 'a scandal of glaring inequalities' (n. 10), a 'stifling materialism' (n. 18) and 'the international imperialism of money' (n. 26, as originally highlighted by Pope Pius XI). In Africa, neither the private and public funds invested, nor the gifts and loans made, have brought peace and development. It is not just a matter of alleviating hunger, nor even of reducing poverty. It is rather a question of a global vision of the human being, a question of building up 'a world where every man, no matter what his race, religion or nationality, can live a fully human life, freed from servitude imposed on him by other men or by natural forces over which he has not sufficient control; a world where freedom is not an empty word' (n. 47).

The building up of the new economic world requires not mere changes but rather bold reforms in three areas, namely, free competition, free trade and debt. First, the 'economy of exchange can no longer be based solely on the law of free competition, a law which, in its turn, too often creates an economic dictatorship' (n. 59). In trade relations between developed and underdeveloped economies, conditions are too disparate and the degrees of genuine freedom available too unequal. The wealth of the rich and the dominion of the strong are increasing, while the poor are left in their misery and the servitude of the oppressed is growing.

Secondly, 'the rule of *free trade*, taken by itself, is no longer able to govern international relations. Its advantages are certainly evident when the parties involved are not affected by any excessive inequalities of economic power' (n. 58). Excessive economic inequalities lead mainly to trade inequalities among industrially developed countries and developing countries. In fact, 'highly industrialised nations export for the most part manufactured goods, while countries with less developed economies have only food, fibres and other raw materials to sell. As a result of technical progress the value of manufactured goods is rapidly increasing and they can always find an adequate market. On the other hand, raw materials produced by underdeveloped countries in Africa are subject to wide and sudden fluctuations in price, a state of affairs far removed from the progressively increasing value of industrial products' (n. 57). It means that the efforts made to assist African developing nations on a financial and technical basis are illusory if their benefits are almost nullified as a consequence of the unequal trade relations existing between rich and poor countries. This is why the rich nations become ever richer while the poor are forever poor.

Thirdly, another consequence of the 'economic dictatorship' is the burden of bilateral and multilateral *debt*. Paul VI rightly states that 'developing countries will no longer risk being overwhelmed by debts whose repayment swallows up the greater part of their gains. Rates of interest and time for repayment of the loan could be so arranged as not to be too great a burden on either party, taking into account free gifts, interest-free or low-interest loans, and the time needed for liquidating the debts. And the receiving countries could demand that there be no interference in their political life or subversion of their social structures' (n. 54).

In the face of these economic challenges, what should be done? In *Populorum Progressio*, the following four main proposals are made:

    (i) reduce and eliminate the excessive inequalities of economic power by keeping the competitive market within the limits that make it just and moral, and therefore human. 'In order that international trade be human and

moral, social justice requires that it restore to the participants a certain equality of opportunity.' (n. 61);

(ii) recognise that 'freedom of trade is fair only if it is subject
to the demands of social justice' (n. 59);

(iii) consider that African 'countries are sovereign states having the right to conduct their own affairs, to decide on
their policies and to move freely towards the kind of society they choose' (n. 85);

(iv) bring about, in commercial exchange between developed
and developing countries, 'a system of cooperation freely
undertaken, an effective and mutual sharing, carried out
with equal dignity on either side, for the construction of a
more human world' (n. 54).

In Africa, as Structural Adjustments Programmes (SAPs) have
not produced expected outcomes, in order to benefit from the
global economy African people have to believe that the upper-
most priority is the right to self-development and to be convinced – along with Joseph Ki-Zerbo – that 'people do not get
developed, but they develop themselves'. It is worth mentioning
that the New Partnership for Africa's Development, NEPAD,[2]
offers a holistic and comprehensive vision, a strategic action
framework that allows African people to participate in integrated
and sustainable socioeconomic development. NEPAD is designed to address the current challenges facing the African continent. Its primary objectives are to:

- engage in good governance as a basic requirement for
  peace, security and sustainable political and socioeconomic development, African ownership and leadership,
  as well as broad and deep participation by all sectors of
  society;
- anchor the development of Africa in its resources and re-
  sourcefulness of its people;
- make efficient and competitive economic regional organisations such as Sadc, Cedao, Comesa, Cemac, for the best
  interests of African peoples, promoting commercial relations within a common market, setting up financial, fiscal,
  and social policies for African nations.
- forge a new international partnership that changes the

unequal relationship between Africa and the developed world;

- ensure that all Partnerships with NEPAD are linked to the Millennium Development Goals and other agreed development goals and targets;
- increase diversification of production and exports, particularly with respect to agro-industries, manufacturing, mining, minerals and tourism. In the agricultural area, we would make headway if, in each African country, on nutritional grounds, we produced what we consumed and if we consumed what we are producing.
- promote policy reforms and increased investment in the following priority sectors: agriculture, human development with a focus on health, education, science and technology and skills development; building and improving infrastructure, including Information and Communication Technology (ICT), energy, transport, water and sanitation;
- achieve a capacity for policy development, coordination and negotiation in the international arena, to ensure Africa's beneficial engagement in the global economy, especially on trade and market access issues.

At the Political Level

African peoples are the first raw material of own their development, of their authentic human development. They have the political right, 'the prime responsibility to work for their own development' (n. 35) in harmony with their social and cultural values. Sustainable development, however, is not to be brought about in isolation. Regional political economic agreements exist among African countries and aim at increasing commercial exchange of goods and services. In this context, NEPAD is an excellent political initiative formally adopted at the 37th Summit of the African Union in July 2001, asking western countries to consider African nations as political and economic partners.

To attain this aim, African peoples have the right to know how international decisions are made within the international financial institutions (World Bank, IMF, and WTO) and in whose interest. This would give them opportunities to express opinions about measures that concern them and provide the possibility to have an input in the design of these measures. With ups and downs, African nations are learning how to implement principles of democracy, good political economic governance, and to ensure the protection of human rights.

We have a sense of being invaded, pillaged and plundered. Conflicts[3] and violence fuelled by a profiting arms trade have ravaged entire countries. Conflicts and civil wars are still going in the eastern part of the Democratic Republic of Congo (DRC), in Rwanda with the interhamwe, in Uganda with the Lord Resistance Army (LRA), in Burundi, in Somalia, in Sudan in the Darfur region, in Chad and in the Central Africa Republic. According to the UN report on the illegal exploitation of natural resources in the DRC, these 'wars are nourished by opportunist alliances and mercenaries, by the damaging effects of globalisation with its political-financial mafias, the constitution of the association of criminals'.[4] Natural resources like oil (Angola), timber (Liberia), diamonds (Angola, DRC, and Sierra Leone), coltan, gold, and other minerals in the DRC have been exploited and traded by multinationals (26 in 1998), governments, armed opposition, and local military commanders in exchange for military supplies and personal financial gain. Internal forces, especially the lack of good governance, the mismanagement of public funds and the existence of a corrupt political elite have reinforced the economic underdevelopment. The African Union, through the Council for Peace and Security[5] should play a more effective role in conflict prevention, in protecting Africa's major interests, and in establishing political stability based on a democratic system of government.

It seems to us that there is a lack of political will and commitment among African leaders to change the situation from which they benefit. One of the main tasks of the political leaders is to promote intelligence in order to transform natural resources. According to Mgr Laurent Monsengwo, 'The Africa of resources is most of all the African person and all that his physical, intellectual, spiritual and moral energies can do to make more human and more harmonious the African social, religious, cultural and physical environment.'[6]

At the Ethical Level

Increased possession of wealth is not the ultimate goal for nations and individuals. Rightly understood, 'full human development' is not a mere economic, social, technological development. It is a development of 'every human being and of the whole human being' (n. 14). It means the promotion of all the dimensions of human being. It implies material, social, economic, cultural and religious development. From the ethical viewpoint, it is mainly a personal and communal development. This personal and communal development would be threatened if the true scale of values were undermined. Individuals, families and nations can be overcome by avarice.[7]

'Values such as hospitality, the sense of the family and of the sacred, a deep religious sense, the love and the respect for life, a great veneration for their ancestors and elders, the sense of feast and of sharing, parental solidarity, are profoundly rooted in the African people.'[8] This cultural vitality is the greatest asset of the African people in their struggle for total liberation and the building of a society capable of facing the problems of our time in a globalised world.

In the present situation, our political, economic, social and religious life is deeply affected by the market-culture.[9] In general, a global economy does not promote people's values in Africa. What is needed is 'a new humanism which will enable modern man to find himself anew by embracing the higher values of love and friendship, of prayer and contemplation' (n. 20). A new humanism rooted in international socioeconomic justice requires that developed countries assume the duty to free themselves for equitable trade and to establish fair relationships with developing countries. 'This duty is the concern especially of better-off nations. Their obligations stem from a brotherhood that is at once human and supernatural, and take on a threefold aspect: the duty of human solidarity, of social justice, of universal charity' (n. 44). Thus integral human development requires a set of values, ethical norms, and moral demands for all nations.

At the Sociocultural Level

Socially, the global economy leads African countries to economic, political and cultural marginalisation that has taken new forms. In the context of a global world apparently promising prosperity to all, 'marginalisation appears as a process denying opportunities and outcomes to those living "on the margins" and enhancing the opportunities and outcomes of those who are "at the centre".'[10] Financial international institutions like the World Bank, the WTO and IMF have increased the effect of globalisation by encouraging and supporting the implementation of market-driven economic policies across the globe. Thus the social impact of the market-culture has a negative impact on African cultural heritage. It reinforces in many ways environmental decay, increased corruption, urban violence, cultural alienation, 'the unbearable burden of the debt, the horror of wars nourished by the traffic of arms without any scruples, the shameful and pitiful spectacle of the refugees and of displaced persons'.[11]

One must recognise that every programme of development, made to increase goods and services, has no other *raison d'être* than the service of human beings. 'Such programmes should reduce inequalities, fight discriminations, free man from various types of servitude and enable him to be the instrument of his own material betterment, of his moral progress and of his spiritual growth. To speak of development is in effect to show as much concern for social progress as for economic growth. And man is only truly man in as far as, master of his own acts and judge of their worth, he is author of his own advancement, in keeping with the nature which was given to him by his Creator and whose possibilities and exigencies he himself freely assumes' (n. 34).

The human being is the alpha and omega of all types of development. Economic growth is at his/her service (n. 27) and depends in the very first place upon social and cultural progress: thus basic education[12] is 'the primary object of any plan of development. It can even be affirmed that economic growth depends in the very first place upon social progress. Indeed hunger for education is no less debasing than hunger for food: an illiterate is a person with an undernourished mind. To be able to read and write, to acquire a professional formation, means to recover confidence in oneself and to discover that one can progress along with the others' (n. 35).

Concerning education, it is urgent to ensure investment in human beings, through quality training and teaching, to implement the establishment of the African Academy of Sciences (a specialised department of the African Union). Strategic and prospective research centres should be created to plan and to anticipate the future in the political, economic, cultural, social and religious areas, because where vision is lacking there is no hope. Ideally cultural, intellectual and scientific heritage should be appropriated and adapted to African society's real needs, to the physical, social, political, and economic environment.

Some voices speak of the need to go back to the the traditional African values of sharing and solidarity, to building new relationships: 'development divorced from its human or cultural context is growth without a soul' (World Commission on Culture and Development, 1995, p. 48). In the last analysis, it is the culture which, as a set of values, gives significance and direction to politics and economics. Culture makes us what we are, and explains what we do. We have the power to reshape the way we live our life together. This is why primacy must be given to African local cultures to preserve against the political and economic homogenisation power of global forces. Africa can draw from the Japanese model where cultural identity and techno-scientific competitiveness go hand in hand.

Peace and Development
The global economy operates within a neoliberal development paradigm, which has produced in Africa neither economic growth nor social progress. As unchecked liberalism leads to the excessive inequalities of economic power (n. 58), 'unmerited misery', in the same way, leads to conflicts, violence and wars.[13] It is not sufficient to increase wealth, and to promote technology to render the world a more human place in which to live. Economics and technology have no meaning except in the context of the human being whom they should serve.

We know that on some crucial issues relating to peace, such as human rights and development, there are different theoretical approaches. 'The urgency to solve issues related to water, education, sanitation and health has resulted in favouring the adoption of a stakeholder approach to resolve conflicts and find solutions'.[14] In *Populorum Progressio*, the approach has a moral emphasis with a special relation to politics and economics. The very first assumption is that there can be no economic development without social peace and security, without political stability.

The consequences of free trade, free competition, and external debt are obstacles to peace. The consequences of the arms trade are morally unacceptable with millions of deaths, millions of refugees and internally displaced persons. A new form of violence, conflict and peace initiatives has emerged with a special intensity in the African continent. Paul VI rightly affirms that 'excessive economic, social and cultural inequalities among peoples arouse tensions and conflicts, and are a danger to peace' (n. 76).

What is morally scandalous and against the recognition of a person's dignity is the process of the arms race. 'The stock-piles of armaments which have been built up in various countries must be reduced all round and simultaneously by the parties concerned. Nuclear weapons must be banned. A general agreement must be reached on a suitable disarmament programme, with an effective system of mutual control' (*Pacem in Terris*, n. 112). Unless this process of disarmament is carried out, it is impossible to stop the arms race, or to reduce and abolish armaments. Political leaders have to realise that true and lasting peace among nations cannot consist in the possession of an equal supply of armaments but only in mutual trust and cooperation.

More profoundly, 'peace is an order that is founded on truth, built up on justice, nurtured and animated by charity, and brought into effect under the auspices of freedom' (*Pacem in Terris*, n. 167). Peace is not the result of negotiations, political compromises or economic bargaining. It cannot be limited to a mere absence of war, the result of an ever precarious balance of forces. 'Peace is something that is built up day after day, in the pursuit of an order intended by God, which implies a more perfect form of justice among men' (*Populorum Progressio*, n. 76).

Peace and development require effective world solidarity, in order to bring about development and peace. It depends mainly on political leaders to see that 'the dangerous and futile rivalry of powers should give place to collaboration which is friendly, peaceful and free of vested interests, in order to achieve a responsible development of mankind, in which all men will have an opportunity to find their fulfilment' (*Populorum Progressio*, n. 84).

What can be done in order to bring about development and to save peace? We can mention the following proposals, mainly from *Populorum Progressio*:

- to be convinced that 'the very life of poor nations, civil peace in developing countries, and world peace itself are at stake' (n. 55);
- to believe that 'the way to peace lies in the area of development' (n. 83);
- 'to wage war on misery and to struggle against injustice is to promote, along with improved conditions, the human and spiritual progress of all men, and therefore the common good of humanity' (n. 76);
- 'to include the task of establishing new relationships for individuals, families, nations, the whole human race ... under the mastery and guidance of truth, justice, charity and freedom, to bring about true peace in accordance with divinely established order' (*Pacem in Terris*, n. 163);
- to work for a cessation of the arms race, of economic inequalities that constitute a danger for peace.

Conclusion

I have tried in this chapter first to give the *status quaestionis* of development in the world and in Africa. Secondly we have clarified *Populorum Progressio*'s vision of development, questioning the emerging challenges at the economic, political, ethical and sociocultural levels. Thirdly we have shown that peace and development are interconnected, that both individuals and peoples have to walk together in order 'to assure a full human enhancement and to take their rightful place with other nations' (n. 6).

In the current situation in Africa, good governance is needed as a basic requirement for peace and security, sustainable political and socioeconomic development. We believe that NEPAD, if implemented, can play a major role in eradicating poverty, in promoting economic growth and social progress, and in halting the marginalisation of Africa in the globalisation process and enhancing its full and beneficial integration into the global economy.

Christ is the one who brings us peace, who bequeaths it to us: 'Peace I leave with you: my peace I give unto you: not as the world gives, do I give unto you.' Christ is also the one who promises and brings to us the fullness of life, the fullness of human development. He is the only one who commits us 'on the road to development that leads to peace' (n. 77).

References

World Commission on Culture and Development (1995), *Our creative diversity*, Paris: UNESCO.

Pope John XXIII (1963) *Pacem in terris*, Encyclical on establishing universal peace in truth, justice, charity, and liberty, 11 April 1963.

Pope Pius XI (1931) *Quadragesimo Anno*, Encyclical on reconstruction of the social order, 15 May 1931.

Notes
1. Pope John Paul II, Apostolic Exhortation, *Ecclesia in Africa*, Medias Paul, 1995, n. 42.
2. For the New Partnership for African Development (NEPAD) see http:/www.nepad.org/. The NEPAD is a strategic framework document arising from a mandate given to the five initiating Heads of State (Algeria, Egypt, Nigeria, Senegal, and South Africa) by the African Union.
3. Conflicts in Northern Uganda are costing the Ugandan economy at least US$100 million every year. Sudan's military budget has more than doubled since construction began on the Red Sea pipeline in 1998, rising from US$94.5 million in 1997 to US$327 million in 2000. Arms were freely imported from many countries in the European Union, Eastern Europe, Russia and China.
4. Security Council, Group of Experts, *The illegal exploitation of natural resources and other riches of DRC*, Report of November 10, 2001, p. 223-224.
5. For the African Union launching of the ECOSOC see http://www.afica.union.org/organs/ecosoc/home.htm.
6. Mgr Laurent Monsengwo Pasinya, 'De l'Afrique des richesses à celle des ressources ' in *Congo-Afrique* 10 (1996) 518.
7. 'Both for nations and individual, avarice is the most evident form of moral underdevelopment' (n. 19).
8. SCEAM, *The Church and human promotion in Africa today*, Pastoral Exhortation, Epiphany, Kinshasa, n. 12.

9. Market-culture means ideas, practices and institutional behaviour that make profit the primary value of humankind.
10. Social Justice Secretariat, *Globalization and Marginalization, our global apostolic response*, Rome, February 2006, n. 33, p. 19. Marginalisation offends human dignity and involves the denial of human rights.
11. Pope John Paul II, *Ecclesia in Africa*, n. 114.
12. As Paul VI said in his message to the UNESCO Congress held in 1965 at Teheran, 'for man literacy is a fundamental factor of social integration, as well as of personal enrichment, and for society it is a privileged instrument of economic progress and of development' (*Documentation catholique*, tome 62, Paris, 1965, colonne 1674-1675. In Africa the billions of dollars spent every year to buy arms should be invested in education.
13. In the words of Pope Pius XII: 'The calamity of a world war, with the economic and social ruin and the moral excesses and dissolution that accompany it, must not on any account be permitted to engulf the human race for a third time.' (*Gaudium et Spes*, n. 85).
14. *Promotio Justitiae*, n. 89, Seeking peace in a violent world. Workshop on violence and war: cultural and economic interests, 2005/4, 6.

Trade Justice for Africa
and Populorum Progressio

Jack Jones Zulu

The efforts which are being made to assist developing nations on a financial and technical basis, though considerable, would be illusory if their benefits were to be partially nullified as a consequence of the trade relations existing between rich and poor countries. The confidence of these latter would be severely shaken if they had the impression that what was being given them with one hand was being taken away with the other. (*Populorum Progressio*, n. 56)

Introduction

The very strong words about the impact of trade relations between rich and poor countries, cited above, were written 40 years ago. But they could just as well have been written today. The truth of their warning has never been more relevant. And they are certainly relevant to our situation in Africa, and in Zambia in particular.

The shocking social statistics that display the plight of Africa today should not hide the tremendous potential of the continent, so rich in natural and human resources. But the facts must be honestly looked at, unpleasant as they are. For it is in the light of these facts that the trade justice issues must be addressed, guided by the values of *Populorum Progressio*.

Nearly half of Africa's population of slightly over 800 million people lives on less than a dollar per day. Of the 1.2 billion people who live in extreme consumption poverty in the world today, 66 per cent are in sub-Saharan Africa. In the world of plenty, millions are still going hungry and many more suffer from dietary deficiencies. Of these, women and children, whose faces are synonymous with poverty and other forms of deprivation, are the most vulnerable. Only 58 per cent of Africa's population has access to clean water. And illiteracy rates for girls above fifteen years stand at 41 per cent.

Every day, 8,200 people all over the world die because of HIV and AIDS-related illnesses. Six thousand of these deaths occur in Africa, particularly south of the Sahara. Of the 40 million HIV cases reported worldwide, 70 per cent are in sub-Saharan Africa, with almost 3 million African cases being children under the age of fifteen years. It is further projected that nearly 90 million Africans could be infected in the next twenty years if nothing is done to combat the pandemic. Meanwhile, every year pharmaceutical companies and cartels declare massive profits reaped from selling patented AIDS drugs in poor countries, especially those in Africa. If current rules protecting patented medicines were to be changed, millions of infected people would have a chance to live longer.

But we who live in Africa know that the HIV / AIDS pandemic is not simply a medical-pharmaceutical challenge or an issue of behavioural change. It is profoundly a development problem, basically a question of justice (Kelly, 2006). It relates to issues such as poverty, education, nutrition, health, stigma and discrimination, gender inequities, power structures, and global socioeconomic structures and practices.

One powerful example of these global structures is the international debt regime. Africa is burdened with an external debt stock of over US$330 billion, mainly owed to multilateral, bilateral and private creditors in the rich North. The continent spends an average of US$15 billion in annual debt service to the international lending institutions – this is four times more than what Africa spends on the education and health sectors combined.

Another powerful example, of course, is the international trade regime, and in what follows, we will look at the role of trade, with a particular focus on the kind of trade justice issues raised very cogently by Paul VI's great document, *Populorum Progressio*.

Trade as a Tool of Development

Over the last fifty years, trade has been a key driver of economic development in the Western world, in Japan, and more recently in China and India. Developing countries, especially in Asia, have used trade to break into new markets and to change the outlook of their economies. Two decades ago, 70 per cent of their trade was in raw materials but today 80 per cent is in manufactured goods. Unfortunately, this is not the case in Africa. Here trade in raw materials continues to dominate the trading patterns of the continent. While trade does not obviate the need for large-scale development investments supported by Official Development Assistance (ODA), an open and equitable trading system can indeed be a powerful driver of economic growth and poverty reduction. This is especially so when combined with adequate aid.

Recognition of the link between trade and aid as important tools for development can be found in the analysis and recommendations offered by Paul VI. He speaks of 'the duty of human solidarity – the aid that the rich nations must give to developing countries; the duty of social justice – the rectification of inequitable trade relations between powerful nations and weak nations' (n. 44).

Development therefore rightly lies at the heart of the World Trade Organisation (WTO) Doha round of multilateral trade negotiations. At present, developing countries are often denied a level playing field to compete in global trade because rich countries use a variety of tariffs, quotas and subsidies to restrict access to their own markets and shelter their own producers.

What we all too often see is that the rich developed countries in the North make grand promises regarding trade, aid and debt, but the less developed countries continue to face very serious problems (IJND, 2005). Examples of this can be found in the current trading situations affecting Africa and other developing areas.

International trade protocols subtly crafted in favour of the developed countries cause untold suffering and poverty for millions of people in Africa, especially small-scale farmers and producers. Agricultural subsidies in developed countries cost US$1 billion per day. If this money were re-allocated for development in poor countries, world poverty would be significantly reduced. For instance, in Japan each cow is subsidised by a payment of US$4; meanwhile, the majority of Africans live on less than a US$1 per day (Commission for Africa, 2005). Moreover, subsidies on cotton produced in USA lower the world prices and immediately affect the livelihoods of poor farmers who are growing cotton in Zambia.

Anglican Archbishop Njongonkulu Ndungane of Cape Town, South Africa, recently noted that 'Developed countries spend a whopping sum of US$350 billion every year to protect their markets through subsidies and tariffs, yet if Africa increased its share of world exports by even one per cent, this would generate US$70 billion.' Such a huge amount of money is almost six times what Africa receives in foreign aid per year.

WTO Negotiations – for Development?

What kind of guidance can *Populorum Progressio* offer to the trade negotiations that would assist the development of countries in Africa? It is important to appreciate that simply more 'free trade' is not going to be the answer. And this was clearly recognised by Paul VI in his critique of this liberal approach in the face of the evolving global situation between rich and poor countries of vastly unequal power:

> In other words, the rule of free trade, taken by itself, is no longer able to govern international relations. Its advantages are certainly evident when the parties involved are not affected by any excessive inequalities of economic power: it is an incentive to progress and a reward for effort. That is why industrially developed countries see in it a law of justice. But the situation is no longer the same when economic conditions differ too widely from country to country: prices which are 'freely' set in the market can produce unfair results. One must recognise that it is the fundamental principle of liberalism, as the rule for commercial exchange, which is questioned here. (n. 58)

It is indeed unfortunate that the December 2005 WTO ministerial meetings missed a chance to map out an agreement on how to correct the anomalies in trade arrangements and direct trade negotiations for development. In recent years there has been much dispute within the WTO over the need to establish a timetable for developed countries to dismantle market access barriers. This would mean a calendar to begin phasing out trade-distorting domestic subsidies, especially in agriculture. To address this priority, the Doha round of multilateral trade negotiations should have fulfilled its development promise in July 2006.

Regrettably, the talks yet again collapsed. Member states, particularly rich countries who should have agreed to provide duty-free and quota-free market access for all exports from the least developed countries, became remarkably reluctant at the eleventh hour. One clear reason for this is that there is a recognisable manipulation of the operations of the WTO by powerful business and commercial interests of the multinational corporations based in rich countries. For them, economic competition is a primary rule that is to be promoted, without hindrance from a development agenda favourable to poor countries. Isn't this exactly the situation described by Paul VI?

> … an economy of exchange can no longer be based solely on the law of free competition, a law which, in its turn, too often creates an economic dictatorship. Freedom of trade is only fair if it is subject to the demands of social justice. (n. 59)

This of course gives rise to a set of very fundamental questions. For example, is the WTO the right forum for promoting fair trade between rich and poor countries? Can the WTO fix the damage that has been inflicted on poor countries by years of unfair trade in Western markets? These questions need candid answers from all of us.

It has to be noted that 70 per cent of Africans directly depend on agriculture for their livelihood. Yet this is a sector that, coupled with the unfair terms of trade it faces in Western markets, is highly susceptible to exogenous shocks such as chronic and persistent droughts. Moreover, the policies of agricultural liberalisation imposed on the continent by the two Bretton Woods Institutions (the International Monetary Fund (IMF) and the World Bank) in the late 1980s and early 1990s – pre-conditions for lending and settlement of debts – caused a trail of suffering among millions of small-scale farmers as they faced stiff competition from rich and commercial farmers in the developed countries.

The IMF and the World Bank, with their firm grip on economic and social policies in Africa and their insistence on 'free market' economies under the guise of the so-called 'Washington Consensus', have literally left African farmers at the mercy of powerful multinational corporations. It is a case of a 'mosquito-weight facing a heavy-weight' in the boxing ring of international trade.

Trade Justice and Good Governance

> There are a lot of ifs and buts on the way to a fairer world. But, if trade took off for the poorest countries ... and if rich nations played fair with poor ones, by allowing them a decent foothold in Western markets ... and if the governments of developing countries ploughed the new revenues back into health and education, back into good governance and improving their infrastructure ... and if they were able to open their markets in their own time ... then many people who are presently poor would no longer be ... and the world would take a giant step towards ending poverty. (*DFID*, 2005)

We cannot effectively talk about trade justice without dealing with issues of global governance. For instance, it is an acknowledged fact that the political and economic interests of G8 nations drive the agenda of the IMF and of the World Bank. Using their financial muscle, which is translated into voting power, these powerful nations literally 'own' the two institutions. All too often, Africa and its many development and poverty interests are left on the periphery of key decisions. Is it fair that Africa with 47 members in the two institutions has only two executive directors on the boards of the IMF and the World Bank while Europe, which is much smaller in geographical and demographic size compared to Africa, has eleven executive directors on the two boards?

Similar governance questions can be raised about the WTO. In theory, the WTO is democratic and each member state has one vote, but in practice the WTO is quite undemocratic and the poor countries are routinely subject to bullying and threats from the powerful nations. These rich countries frequently use their aid portfolios to intimidate poor and weaker nations into signing bad trade protocols. A look at the records of recent gatherings of the WTO reveals this fact. And the words of *Populorum Progressio* have a prophetic ring:

> In trade between developed and underdeveloped economies, conditions are too disparate and the degrees of genuine freedom available too unequal. In order that international trade be human and moral, social justice requires that it restore to the participants a certain equality of opportunity. (n. 61)

It is not only in the formal gatherings of the WTO in Doha or Hong Kong or other international venues that the unequal conditions are felt and poor countries are sometimes excluded from key decision-making processes. Currently over thirty developing countries have no formal negotiator at the WTO headquarters in Geneva. And many other countries have only one negotiator. Zambia would be an example of the latter situation. This negotiator faces an impossible task of attending over eighty WTO monthly meetings, meetings that are well prepared by the teams of multiple negotiators representing the rich countries.

If there is no change in these democratic deficits in the global institutions of governance, how can the world move toward a fair trade regime? It is simply not possible.

Free Trade versus Fair Trade
To return to the fundamental teaching of *Populorum Progressio* on trade relationships, the content and consequences of free trade is what is being questioned – not only 40 years ago but certainly today also. 'Freedom of trade is fair only if it is subject to the demands of social justice' (n. 59).

In discourse and decisions in trade circles such as the WTO, or in the negotiations between Europe and Africa under the Cotonou Agreement, the rich countries tend to utilise very enticing words to claim that free trade – no subsidies or domestic protection – is the key to escaping poverty. This would be found, for example, in the arguments around the Economic Partnership Agreements (EPAs) being negotiated between the European Union and African states. The logic states: we in Europe will open up our markets to your exports if you open up your markets to our exports.

However, the trouble with this kind of logic is that when poor countries in Africa, Latin America and Asia open up their markets to foreign competition through free trade, they let in powerful foreign firms that enjoy huge market advantages. Local companies simply cannot compete favourably. Experience in a number of countries has so far shown that countries which rapidly opened up their markets to free trade – for example, Haiti, Nepal, Peru, Mali, Zambia – have very poor records of economic growth and poverty reduction. Simply visit Zambia and see the evidence of this.

On the other hand, countries that have reduced poverty through trade such as the South East Asian countries (South Korea, Taiwan, Singapore, Thailand, for example) have grown precisely because they have been able to manage their economic development and have not necessarily used free trade policies as championed by the trio of the IMF, the World Bank and the WTO. For this reason, we repeat the injunction of Paul VI: 'In other words, the rule of free trade, taken by itself, is no longer able to govern international relations' (n. 58).

Conclusion

This analysis strongly contends that international trade, if carried out under right conditions, can be a powerful vehicle for economic growth and subsequently vital for poverty reduction. However, the current trade regime is permeated by unfair trade practices that favour developed countries at the expense of developing countries, especially in Africa.

Three obvious policy recommendations come from this analysis:

First, it is right that governments in the poor South be given wider policy space to choose the best solutions to end poverty and protect their environment. Developed countries should desist from imposing harmful policy conditionality including trade liberalisation that damages the livelihoods of poor countries. The world should instead begin to move toward a fair trade regime that takes into account the varying degrees of individual country development. 'Free market' policies under the wholesale process of liberalisation, privatisation and deregulation should be revisited in light of the emerging evidence about the rising social, economic and environmental costs across the world. 'Without abolishing the competitive market', advises Paul VI, 'it should be kept within the limits which make it just and moral, and therefore human' (n. 61).

Second, the developing countries themselves should seek greater cooperation – so-called 'South-South' arrangements and regional accords – to promote their development. In the words of *Populorum Progressio*, the developing countries should 'take advantage of their proximity in order to organise among themselves, on a broadened territorial basis, areas for concerted development; to draw up programmes in common, to coordinate investments, to distribute the means of production, and to organise trade' (n. 64). That is happening with Zambia's participation in such regional groups as the Southern African Development Community (SADC) and the Common Market for Eastern and Southern Africa (COMESA).

Third, there is need for civil society organisation – churches, trade unions, business groups, human rights groups – to organise and campaign for more fair trade practices. Just as the global Jubilee 2000 movement did tremendous work to promote cancellation of the huge and destructive external debts of poor countries, so there should be a wide movement to advocate for changes in a trade regime that is also destructive of poor countries' efforts to improve the lives of their citizens. This requires good analysis, popular mobilisation and solid moral foundations. As is evident in what has been outlined in this article, *Populorum Progressio* continues to provide great help in laying that solid moral foundation.

References

Commission for Africa (2005) *Our Common Interest: Report of the Commission for Africa*, London: Commission for Africa.

Department for International Development (DFID) (2005) *Trade Matters in the Fight Against World Poverty*, London: Department for International Development.

IJND (International Jesuit Network for Development) (2005) *Debt and Trade: Time to Make the Connections*, Dublin: Veritas.

Kelly, Michael J. (2006) *HIV and AIDS: A Justice Perspective*, Lusaka: Jesuit Centre for Theological Reflection.

The Debt Problem and the
Response of Latin American Civil Society

Rómulo Torres Seoane

The encyclical *Populorum Progressio* developed a series of ideas in order to help prevent the negative effects for national development that could have resulted from the commercial and financial relationships that evolved since the end of the 1960s. The encyclical warned about what could happen regarding massive debt, political impositions, and new dependencies that would mean a descent into a neo-colonialism, unless certain courses of action were taken. In this context, it was very important to focus on justice in financial and commercial transactions. However, key events from the 1980s onwards regarding the debt crisis, and the structural adjustment programmes that followed, meant that the scenario we were being warned about had come to pass.

The Pontifical Commission of Peace and Justice prepared a document in 1986, at John Paul II's request, called *At the service of the human community*. It was 'an ethical consideration of international debt' that suggested facing up to the debt crisis to avoid making the same mistake again. This was in line with the ideas in *Populorum Progressio*. His 1987 encyclical on human development, *Sollicitudo rei socialis*, which marked the 20th anniversary of the publication of *Populorum Progressio*, reinforced the same theme: that in the previous two decades 'the chosen instrument to help development had become a counterproductive one'. These considerations were not taken into account, however, in the way we would have liked. Neo-liberalism was already firmly established and the fears of Paul VI were realised.

In the last few years, there have been some reductions in the debt of the poorest countries. There has also been rebalancing of the debt of some 'middle' income countries. This only amounts to temporary, provisional solutions, however, rather than something substantial enough to deal with the problem. The conditions attached to these reductions force these countries' economies to become absorbed into the international market economy. At the same time, there are a number of proposals from international bodies to renegotiate the debt, in order to avoid a crisis, and to promote 'good' development of business and investment. Nonetheless, the crisis continues. In parallel, many social movements continue to struggle, not only on the question of debt, but for the transformation of the economies that exclude huge sectors of the world's population.

Through the international debt movement, civil society has won many victories. On the one hand, the impossibility of repaying the debt as it currently exists is now evident. So too is the 'dominance' relationship that sustains it. On the other hand, strategies have been developed to push policy-makers for structural change, long-term solutions, and global solidarity.

Populorum Progressio, the Debt Crisis and the Church Contribution to an Ethical Approach

The important ideas in *Populorum Progressio* include abandoning unjust structures, an escape from 'slavery', promotion of international solidarity, and highlighting social problems as global issues.

Paul VI starts the second part of the encyclical by affirming:

- The development of an individual cannot happen without the development of human solidarity.
- The assistance of rich nations is a duty of solidarity.
- Correcting flawed commercial relationships between strong and weak countries is an obligation of social justice.
- Making the world more 'human' for everyone is a demand of universal compassion.

This involves dealing with development through the demands of solidarity, justice and compassion, arising from an awareness of global interdependency, and allied to the value of each human. They challenge the unjust reality of the coexistence of rich and poor countries that is brought about by unjust commercial relationships.

Clearly all these ideas have their origin in the concept of development spelt out in the first part of *Populorum Progressio*: to change conditions from less human to more human. This involves challenging oppressive structures that promote the abuse of power and capitalism, ranging from the exploitation of workers to unjust commercial transactions.

The encyclical has, as its main concern, the achievement of stable social development, and an even playing field for business transactions. The problem of justice in trade is highlighted in the encyclical through the following reflections on agreements, debt, and national sovereignty.

Regarding agreements:
- Bilateral and multilateral agreements must continue to exist.
- They allow for the transformation of 'dependency' relationships and the suffering that emerged during the colonial era.
- Within a context of global cooperation they are not to be seen as inherently 'bad'.
- They help to avoid neo-colonialism, i.e. political pressure and economic domination.

Regarding dialogue, debt and political interference:
- There should be dialogue between those who give and those who receive.
- The future risk of being crushed by debt should be avoided, the repayment of which often negates any benefits.
- Interest rates and repayment terms for loans must be agreed and affordable.
- The beneficiaries should insist that there is no political interference, and that it does not affect their social structure.

Regarding national sovereignty and the exchange economy:
- As sovereign states, developing countries have to be in charge of their own affairs and be free to decide on policy and to work towards the kind of society they desire.
- The efforts that have been made at a financial level would be an illusion if the results were partially cancelled out by the nature of commercial relations between rich and poor countries.
- An exchange economy cannot continue to rely on only

one principle, free trade, which in the long-term will create an economic dictatorship.

- Free trade is only fair if it is in accordance with the demands of social justice.

In these ideas we can see clearly the dangers of 'dependency' relationships, the pitfalls of neo-liberalism, the effects of crushing debt, and also the risk of political interference. These are linked to the consequences for social structure, the right to political self-determination, and respecting the direction that society itself has chosen. Another major concern is the possibility of undermining the results of financial planning through commercial relationships. It is assumed that free trade is subject to the demands of social justice, but it seems to merely create economic dictatorship. Again, this is the issue of justice in business.

From our viewpoint today, we can see that the 1967 encyclical was completely ignored by those in power over the last 40 years, as all the things which were supposed to be avoided have actually happened.

The over-indebtedness of Southern hemisphere countries was induced by Northern interests, creating a 'debt addiction' in Southern economies that ended up hindering rather than helping development. The process is as follows: the debt firstly becomes something crushing, and then its renegotiation allows the introduction of policies that mean a loss of autonomy in development. Therefore, the result is that a large part of the population ends up in poverty and unemployed or emigrating.

The condition to renegotiate the debt was the application of the structural adjustment that meant that the state's role would be reduced, as well as the reduction of public expenditure and social spending. At the same time, there was the introduction of privatisation, labour flexibility, liberalisation of trade, and the flow of capital. These allowed the predominance of the demand and supply law, which is considered the best management of resources, and then private initiative supposedly becomes efficient in managing the state's resources.

The 1980s crisis
The crisis caused an unfavourable environment for indebted

countries, a crisis that was characterised by unstable and floating exchange rates, changes in interest rates, and protectionism. The sharp rise in interest rates that happened in the early 1980s increased already massive debts. This had devastating social effects due to cuts in public spending on education, health and other areas. The medium-term consequences included a fall in national savings, postponement of real debt reform, and growth of consumption over investment. The adjustments needed to pay the debt included a fall in imports, changes in the economy, the flight of capital, and a brain drain.

The Paper of the Council for Justice and Peace and Justice Commission Paper

Faced with the debt crisis, John Paul II asked the Pontifical Council for Justice and Peace to produce a position paper based on *Populorum Progressio* and in the spirit of Vatican II. The document was called *At the service of the human community: an ethical approach to the international debt question*. It looked at the pressing problem of the debtor countries' inability to pay. It claimed that debt highlights economic interdependency and limitations on the flow of capital.

It helps to prove that far from being an advantage, we have seen unemployment, recession, and a fall in living standards. The document shows that the poor and middle classes are the main victims, that the situation is intolerable, and that it will affect the creditors in the medium-term. The document claims that faced with this reality, the ethical problem that arises is that servicing the debt cannot be at the price of economic 'suffocation', and that no government can allow its people suffer hardship as a result. In this sense, it makes a call on behalf of the church to the international community that they analyse the ethical implications of the debt, in order to find fair and just solutions which respect people's dignity. It also gives rise to the following ethical principles:

- Creation of a new sense of solidarity.
- Acceptance of co-responsibility.
- Establishing relationships of trust.
- Enabling the participation of all.

Regarding emergency measures, it suggests dialogue and coop-eration; that a 'survival ethic' guide behaviour and decisions; and that unsustainable terms should not be imposed on insol-vent debtors. Even though legal, these requirements can still be abusive. It underlines that from the gospel point of view, mora-toriums and the total or partial cancellation of debts should be considered.

In 1987, *Sollicitudo rei socialis* emphasised the scope of the problem:

> Circumstances have changed, both within the debtor nations and in the international financial market; the instrument chosen to make a contribution to development has turned into a counterproductive mechanism. This is because the debtor nations, in order to service their debt, find themselves obliged to export the capital needed for improving or at least maintaining their standard of living. It is also because, for the same reason, they are unable to obtain new and equally essential financing. (n. 19)

As a way out of the debt problem, some structural adjustment measures were taken as mentioned above. However, free mar-ket and investment liberalisation resulted. The obligations of creditors to debtors were only taken into account in 2000. This followed a debate brought on by the second big debt crisis in the 1990s, and the momentum created by the international coalition 'Jubilee 2000', whose slogan was 'life before debt'.

Official Solutions

From 1995 to 2005 new measures were used to deal with debt. Financial organisations started to differentiate between devel-oping countries on a *per capita* income basis. The measures, which were discussed at G8 meetings, highlighted that previous solutions were inadequate, with an implied recognition that it is impossible to repay the debt in full. However, debt renegoti-ation and conditionality transformed the economies of debtor nations, and highlighted their dependency. Among the first measures was the 1985 Baker Plan. This plan was to help im-prove debtors' financial liquidity through new loans. In 1987, partial repayments were introduced through a market mechan-ism called the 'Options Menu'. This allowed for repurchasing of the debt and its conversion into capital, or social and environ-mental investment.

In 1989 the Brady Plan was established to transform the debt into new premiums; the way out of the problem was seen as the exchanging of old debts for new ones. At the same time, bilateral business negotiations were established on a creditor to creditor basis. These talks took place at the Paris Club under the scrutiny of the International Monetary Fund (IMF).

Faced with the new debt crisis during the 1990s, the G7 asked the World Bank and the IMF for a comprehensive solution. This led to the Heavily Indebted Poor Countries (HIPC) proposal. The beneficiaries of this initiative were to be countries with an income of less than US$800 per capita, which met a series of financial criteria. The debt could be reduced by up to 80 per cent, subject to certain conditions.

Civil Society Intervention and its Results

Faced with the debt crisis of the 1980s, ideas came from the Southern hemisphere as much as from the North. In the Andean region in Latin America, the Andean Forum for Debt and Development (FONDAD) was set up. This space for reflection helped find relevant solutions, through intellectuals such as Oscar Ugarteche and Alberto Acosta, and key organisations such as CEDLA (Bolivia), CEDAL and DESCO (Peru), and ILDIS (Ecuador). In the 1990s then, Eurodad and CADTM were set up in Europe, and Afrodad in Africa.

In 1994, the Debt and Development Forum in Peru was organised, led by the Episcopal Commission of Social Action (CEAS) and the Solidarity Forum (Peru). CEAS would co-ordinate their campaign with the slogan 'Life before Debt'. In Honduras FOS-DEM was established. Together with Eurodad, it started analysis of the emerging HIPC proposal. This effort was supported by Cardinal Rodriguez Maradiaga. In Brazil, a 'social week' was organised around the debt until the end of the 1990s.

The inspiration from the church's social teaching helped members of the church get involved in looking for solutions. This participation was reinforced by John Paul II through *Tertio Millennio Adveniente*, in which he asked the richest countries to cancel the debt to mark the arrival of the second millennium.

This was the beginning of working towards the realisation of the biblical 'jubilee year' in a global context.

In the North, CIDSE-Caritas International suggested cancelling the debt for year 2000, linking this to investment in human development, and improving the HIPC initiative. They also called for transparency in decisions about debt cancellation, and a change to the structure of international financial relationships.

All these initiatives were the beginning of what would later be called Jubilee 2000. This international movement managed to unite different groups working on the issue, to influence G8 decisions on debt. National approaches were channelled into an international movement in a coordinated way. The 'jubilee networks' were born in the Northern and Southern hemispheres through national campaigns.

In Peru, Bolivia, and Brazil, the Episcopal conferences were very important in the campaigns. In Peru, the campaign was coordinated by CEAS, which had thousands of volunteers collecting signatures around churches, factories, universities, and public places. Workshops were organised to help people understand the problem better and its impact on daily life. Regional workshops also developed proposals for alternative development in different areas.

A wide range of civil institutions and organisations cooperated through the Debt and Development Forum of Peru (which CEAS was coordinating at the time). They organised Jubilee Network Peru, whose goals were active participation in the process, interacting with other countries in the campaign and creating solidarity among Northern and Southern societies. Through this movement, national and global groups began a systematic participation in addressing the debt issue through mobilisation, demonstrations, proposing solutions, and consciousness-raising.

Results of Pressure and Mobilisation

The G8 approved a 'Reworked Framework' for the HIPC proposals for 41 countries in Cologne in 1999. The definition of unsustainable debt was broadened, and reductions of 90 per cent were possible. Reduction of poverty was an objective, through the promotion of the 'Poverty Reduction Plan' (PRSP). Other conditions remained in place.

In spite of widespread official recognition that huge debt reductions were needed, and that entry requirements to the scheme should be minimal, many countries were excluded from the proposal. Those which were included had to meet conditions that meant yet more sacrifices for the country in question. Pressure alone was not enough: much more effort was needed, as the powerful did not give up easily, despite having the solution in their hands. For this reason, new campaigning strategies were adopted, and some groups were dissolved while others were set up.

Follow-up with Latin America and Global Society
A new international organisation, Southern Jubilee, was born by bringing together networks and groups from Africa, South America, and Asia. Its aim was to denounce the illegitimacy of the debt, and call for its total cancellation. In Latin America, the 'Andean strategy' was created in Peru, Brazil, Ecuador, and Bolivia. The initial aim was to increase participation and citizen control regarding the debt and social spending. It also dealt with non-payment of the debt and the problem of corruption in its application. The international movement kept up pressure on the financial institutions and the G8, and played an important role in bringing together movements at the World Social Forum, which was set up in Porto Alegre in 2001.

In Peru, members of religious groups who were part of Jubilee Network there – evangelical, Methodist, Presbyterian, Anglican, Lutheran, Orthodox, Islamic, and Catholic – organised ecumenical events to express an ethical view of the injustices perpetrated. Organisations working on the rights of child workers, women, workers, farmers, and citizens, continued to explore the problem within their own training courses, and to make it part of their campaigns. Debt was a key subject within the training programmes of some Regional Conferences for Social Development (COREDES) and forums on poverty.

Follow-up from the Andean Region
The negotiations to restructure the debt resulted in a divergence of approach between the countries of Latin America. Individual

approaches by governments have not provided for a comprehensive solution, because some countries have been categorised
as 'low income' while the majority are termed 'medium income'.
The common factor uniting them is that all have applied the
policies of structural adjustment, with some variations. Jubilee
South America, the regional chapter of the Southern Jubilee,
took on the task of furthering debate on the illegitimacy of the
debt, the promotion of civil debt conversations, and to address
the relationship between debt and free trade agreements.

Follow-up from the Church Network
The CIDSE/Caritas International position in 2002 on debt was:
pushing for greater debt relief; revising the concept of the debt
sustainability, to include poverty levels in the sustainability criteria; cancellation of 100 per cent of the multilateral debt for the
poorest countries; and looking at the insolvency issue, and the
fair and transparent arbitration of debt. They called for the IMF
and the WB to relinquish their power to approve Reduction of
Poverty Programmes (PRSPs). They also sought clarity about
the concept of 'pro-poverty growth', which transforms the concept and practice of structural adjustment, in order to break the
connection between reducing the debt and PRSP; instead, civil
society would take a key role in the approval of PRSPs.

Educational materials were produced by Jesuits for Debt Relief
and Development (JDRAD). More recently, JDRAD evolved to
become the International Jesuit Network on Development
(IJND), with a broader remit including issues of trade, economic
solidarity and governance, thus allowing for an integrated approach to these problems.

*Debate in the Monterrey Conference on Finance for Development and
the G8*
The Monterrey meeting of world leaders discussed the debt
problem as one of six subjects. Among its conclusions were that
further measures were needed, including cancellation, and extra
resources for poorer countries, new mechanisms for medium-
income countries. However, the 'Washington consensus' emerged,
placing emphasis on two factors to achieve development and
end poverty: these were market liberalisation, and the promo-

tion of foreign investment, as well as the management of a 'good' macroeconomic policy. An important suggestion was that each country must develop a 'value' market, as a way of promoting the escape from debt.

The G8 meeting in Evian shortly afterwards authorised the Paris Club to take into account the Monterrey conclusions on debt sustainability, and to adapt solutions to the financial situation of the debtor countries. The countries that were in serious financial trouble could benefit from a broader treatment of the debt issue through reprogramming the flows, changing the profile of the debt, and its reduction.

The Evian focus opened new possibilities for medium-income countries, but in practice these were only accessible through the financial market. The much hoped-for action for these countries, with high levels of poverty and inequality, amounted to a re-profiling of the debt. This meant that the old debt is paid, and a new one acquired by issuing sovereign bonds or payments in advance, as well as an increase of internal debt through government bonds. There was little interest in new debt solutions.

Debt: Finance for Developmentand the Prevention of Crisis, and the Response of World Capital

The 'Monterrey Consensus' and what came after indicated what priorities were applied to managing debt and economic issues. Political events since 2001 had an important role too. To avoid the possibility of a new crisis, reform of the financial system was begun in 2003. The key aims included recognising systemic vulnerabilities regarding debt, and strengthening the monitoring and guidance of development support. Better coordination of regional and multilateral monitoring was also an aim, and establishing a general framework to resolve the crisis in capital accounts.

There is an evaluation of the debt 'load', and of the capacity of countries to take it on. Along with this, a new analytic framework is planned for the emerging market countries (which are at the medium-income level), to create better policies for getting loans, and in order to give guidance to both debtors and creditors on the level of debt reduction, in terms of IMF resource monitoring. Its emphasis is to measure the ability to respond to crisis. It underlines the necessity of measuring the possibility of indefinite maintenance of the initial surplus, and the risk of renewal of the debt.

From there on, official documents talk about the need for careful management of external debt in medium-income countries, to avoid a crisis that could affect the global economy. Also, debt relief for the countries with low income is referred to, and its appropriate management in order to achieve the Millennium Development Goals. In other words, official organisations are focused on crisis prevention – a crisis that could be caused by medium-income countries, given their increasing importance for commerce and global investment. So it becomes a priority for international organisations to manage debt well, to ensure that some finance is available to reduce poverty. Both approaches are needed for the process of trade liberalisation and investment.

Today we are seeing the promotion of Free Trade Agreements and bilateral investment as other ways of applying the WTO agenda. Along with these are offers of new loans to increase trade, achieving good governance, fighting corruption, and reducing vulnerability to crisis.

Debt and how to manage it, continue to be key questions in developing economies. They still have negative balances, for a variety of reasons: the difference between income through investment and wages, and outgoings on services, payment of the debt, and accumulation of reserves.

Until now, the debt has been 'administered' in spite of the unmet needs of the people due to the high price of exports, and because the rate of interest has not grown much. All this allows poverty to continue increasing. There is a minority of people who are satisfied, while the majority lives with growing frustration, and sees migration to developing countries as the only way out.

Challenge for Civil Society:
Developing Fair Economic Relationships
The current situation in Latin America is characterised by the following:

- Economic development sustained in favourable international conditions.
- Poverty.
- Inequality.
- Frustration and growing conflict between sectors.
- Demonstrations against foreign investment and Free Trade Agreements, and in favour of budgets that meet the needs of the different sectors of the population.
- Mistrust of traditional party politics, and a search for new political direction.
- Emigration.
- Partial development of alliances between governments.

The situation of public debt in the region is as follows:
- The total amount of external debt has increased, and is now one of the highest in developing regions.
- The amount spent on servicing this debt has also increased.
- The burden of external debt has decreased through economic growth, control of the fiscal deficit, and revaluations of the exchange rate.
- Internal debt has increased.
- Latin America's public debt has a nation product to debt ratio of 52.25 per cent.

Faced with this situation, Latin American social networks are developing integrated approaches to the debt problem, and the economic and financial mechanisms that create exclusion. The Latin American Network on Debt, Development and Rights (LATINDADD) – the new name for the Andean-Central American-Amazon Strategy – has put forward strategies to resolve the debt problem and the 'exclusive' nature of the economy. It begins with the experience of the international social movements, which were themselves a consequence of the debt problem. They were presented during the Edinburgh G8 summit, and involve three main strategies.

The first is to reinforce the international social base to build an economy based on fair and just service to people, and for a definitive resolution of the external debt problem. It would include the following:

1. The development of the global solidarity movement for the cancellation of the debt, with organisations from all continents. The task calls for training and upskilling of organisations and citizens; getting commitment from political parties to changing actual conditions on the ground; the search for real commitment from the governments of the Southern hemisphere to meet people's demands; and the involvement of civil movements from the South, North, and the governments of the South.
2. The creation of ethical tribunals.
3. The promotion of civil 'listening' forums.

The second is to promote a normative and institutional framework at international level for economic-financial and legal issues, which ensures the final resolution of the external debt problem and the underlying problems that created it. This would involve:

1. Critique of the proposals on sustainability of external debt and the search for autonomy in defining policies on production and trade.
2. 'Legalisation' of the debt issue through taking cases to international courts of human rights violations (relating to health, education, and living standards) caused through paying the external debt. These would be based on international agreements and would involve the presentation of cases of corruption in the acquisition of debt, or arbitrary increases in interest rates.
3. Promotion of an international financial code.

The third strategy is to promote financial mechanisms for the integrated development of countries, allowing for civil participation, as an alternative to the current mechanisms of domination and inequality. This would include:

1. Local and trade union organisations to produce alternative proposals for the national budget, and to participate in monitoring it.
2. The same organisations to develop proposals on their governments' bilateral negotiations, with increased legal pressure, and participation in monitoring them.
3. The monitoring by social movements of private and public investment, and of trade negotiations.

4. The development of a cooperative economy based on solidarity.

Conclusions

Forty years after its publication, *Populorum Progressio* can in effect be seen as a warning of what could happen in financial and
commercial systems. It made its case very clearly, and sought
ways of building instead social, sustainable development. Those
with the power to influence public politics, such as the G8 and
the international financial institutions, have only increased the
liberalisation of investment and trade, which has created more
poverty, inequality and new dependencies. However, the development of a global civil society with more influence has denounced this grave situation, and produced proposals to manage the economy in a different way, with greater involvement of
social movements and citizens in general. In part, the integration
of civil society has been inspired by *Populorum Progressio* and its
legacy.

The fight for social change and a definitive resolution of the debt
problem has been inspired by the Utopian vision of a new society
which needs to be nourished with values from *Populorum
Progressio*. These values will give more coherence to the strategies
that are being set out. The values are human dignity; solidarity;
accountability and participation; respect for the global good; exercise and monitoring of human rights; and co-responsibility.

At the same time we must ask a number of reflective questions:
- How have we advanced the restoration of human dignity?
- Have we removed the shackles that prevent equal oppor-
tunities and the exercise of human rights?
- Has the burden of the external debt been reduced?
- Have the preconditions linked to debt reduction been
eliminated?
- Are the 'indicators for development' taken into account in
making decisions?
- Are the resources of developing countries still being un-
fairly exploited?
- What about protection of the earth and ecology?

- What is the state of solidarity in North-South and South-South relationships, and within each country?
- Are conditions generally becoming more human instead of less human?

References
Pope John Paul II (1987) *Sollicitudo rei socialis* (Concern for Social Realities), papal encyclical.

Insights from Populorum Progressio and the Debate on Governance and Development

Miguel González Martín

Introduction

Governance has emerged over the last few years as one of those unavoidable expressions in the development jargon. Today governance is regarded as one of the most relevant factors explaining the success or failure of development efforts of developing countries. One can hardly find an official document addressing development issues that does not mention good governance or democratic governance as prerequisites for successful development. Most official aid donors treat governance either as an explicit objective of their disbursements or allocation criteria for their funds, or both.[1]

This relevance attached to governance is new to some extent, but is it really new? It appears that the presence of the word 'governance' in the development debate can be traced back no more than 15 years. Nonetheless, most of the issues that today are clustered together under the generic umbrella of 'governance' are deeply rooted in the development debate since its inception, some 60 years ago.

It does not come as a surprise, therefore, that no trace of the word 'governance' is to be found in *Populorum Progressio*. Neither is it in *Sollicitudo Rei Socialis*, written 20 years later, in 1987. The latter tries to update the fundamental insights of the former in a different international context. While *Populorum Progressio*, in spite of challenging the mainstream ideas of development of the period, somehow shares the optimism dominant at that time that the newly independent countries could rapidly catch up with the developed countries, *Sollicitudo Rei Socialis* affirms the failure of the two competing economic and political systems – capitalism and communism – when tackling the problems of development.

We certainly cannot be sure that if a new encyclical on development was written in 2007, 'governance' would appear among its prominent analytical categories or not. It may well be an expression peculiar to development practitioners and scholars. With or without the use of the word, however, the underlying problems and realities would be present, the way they were in the aforementioned encyclicals.

In this chapter I intend to firstly examine how 'governance' came to be relevant in development practice and discourse; secondly, how two different agendas of governance, stressing different features, can be found nowadays; and, thirdly, how the insights of *Populorum Progressio* are closer to one of those agendas than to the other.

The Emergence of the Governance Agenda

The statement that governance and institutions matter for development could hardly be challenged today, but that wasn't clear not so long ago. It is well known that the strategy promoted by the International Financial Institutions (IFI) during the 1980s and part of 1990s was based on the neoliberal belief that free markets are the main and foremost tool for growth, development and welfare. Those beliefs were summarised in the so-called 'Washington Consensus'. The idea of getting prices right was at the centre of that strategy. For that to happen, the market must not suffer any distortion that would hinder its free work. State institutions and policies were seen to be at the root of all evils, impairing the expansion and proper functioning of markets. Therefore, policies oriented towards minimising the influence of the state were put in place. The state, indeed, was regarded as part of the problem.

How can the change of trend be explained? What factors have prompted it? Two elements help explain the shift: practical and theoretical. In reality, both are intrinsically linked, but for analytical purposes it is useful to separate them. For practical reasons, it was obvious that the policies inspired by the 'Consensus' didn't work. They didn't spur growth and poverty reduction in the way it was intended. D. Rodrik (1999) points to three specific situations that brought policy makers to rethink the role of governance and institutions: (i) the failure of privatisation and price reforms in Russia in the absence of a political, legal and regulatory framework; (ii) the disappointment with the results produced by market reforms in Latin America and, (iii) the Asian financial crisis, that showed how liberalisation before regulation leads to disaster.

Not only did the policies of the 'Consensus' not bring sustainable economic growth, in many places they had severe social consequences by neglecting and weakening institutions that acted as cushions during adjustment programmes. Little by little it became clear that the lack of consideration of institutional arrangements was among the more prominent flaws in economic and development policy design. Mainstream economists took for granted the existence of those institutional requirements without which no market can work. The collision of neoliberal economics with developing countries shed light on, for instance, the relevance of a legal framework that protects property rights or the need of a judicial system that enforces contracts.

Currently, it is widely recognised that the exclusion of institutions and, more specifically, the weakening of the state, was a mistake, but there is no agreement when assessing the scope of that mistake. For some, there was a failure in the implementation of the 'Consensus', but nothing wrong *per se* with its contents. F. Fukuyama (2004) argues that the problem lay in the confusion of two dimensions of statehood: scope and strength. Whereas the 'Consensus' policies were intended to reduce the scope of the state, they ended up eroding its strength. Adequate measures would have limited the scope of the state while simultaneously strengthening it. There is no need for a 'minimum state'; instead, development requires an 'effective state'. For others, the problems of the 'Consensus' were not only ones of implementation, but of content too. According to this opinion, state regulation is needed in the realms where the market on its own is not able to promote development. Tax policies, transparency policies, policies for competitiveness and so on were beyond the scope of the 'Consensus' and, nonetheless, are extremely important for development. Finally, we find another set of critiques that challenge more profoundly the idea of development underlying the 'Consensus', namely, its identification of development with efficiency and economic growth. They place a question mark over the *ends* of the consensus. We will return later to this topic.

At the theoretical level, we must mention the influence of neo-institutional economics, specially the work of the economist, Douglass North. This school explains the historical process of market extension as a process of institutional improvement. Institutions matter because their level of development determines the cost of exchanges. The more developed the institutions, the less the transaction costs and uncertainty. From this conception stems the idea of a regulatory state, arbitrator of the rules of the market. However, nothing about a political regime can be derived from this theory.[2] We are in the realm of bureaucratic and administrative effectiveness.

Another theoretical contribution that has helped raise the question of institutions and political arrangements is the human development paradigm, nurtured by the work of Amartya Sen. Sen argues that 'individuals live and operate in a world of institutions. Our opportunities and prospects depend crucially on what institutions exist and how they function. Not only do institutions contribute to our freedoms, their roles can be sensibly evaluated in the light of their contributions to our freedom. To see development as freedom provides a perspective in which institutional assessment can systematically occur' (2000: 178). The idea that democratic rights and participation are part of the definition of development, stem from the notion of 'development as freedom'. Therefore, the mission of the state is not only to provide a hotbed for the market; state institutions are responsible for the fulfilment of citizens' rights and for providing basic services. While neo-institutionalism stresses the 'effective state', the human development approach underscores the 'accountable state' for citizens' demands, some of them articulated as rights.

In short, after two decades of absence, the state receives again attention as an important actor in development. However, this return to the scene does not mean that it occupies centre stage. This is by no means the resurrection of the 'developmental state' of the 1950s and 1960s. The state has to share its prominence with two other key actors: the market and civil society. It is precisely in this context of rethinking the role of the state that the term of 'governance' comes into the debate. The term had been employed in different areas of social and political sciences, especially in a Western context, in order to refer to the various dimensions of state crisis: the crisis of the welfare state, the blurring of limits between public and private, the incapacity of the state in the face of emerging global and local powers (Graña, 2005). Hence, 'governance' would be used to mean horizontal and participatory modalities in management, as opposed to the centralised and interventionist state. According to this vision, several actors (the private sector, experts, civil society ...) would take part in decision making, along with public officials, to tackle a range of problems of growing complexity and interconnectedness. We could say that the idea of 'governance' came in handy when rethinking the role of the state in the context of developing countries.

It is probably this mixed array of theoretical and practical sources that makes the term 'governance' so difficult to grasp. In spite of some good definitions and research highlighting its relevance for development, we cannot avoid the strong impression that we are dealing with another buzzword in development jargon. Different actors invest the term with different meanings. As A. Cornwall and K. Brock (2005) have pointed out, particular combinations of buzzwords appear linked in development policies. As a result of this phenomenon, the meaning of the term relies heavily on the other words accompanying it, on the connection between them and on who is voicing them. The case of 'governance' is a clear example. Configuring 'governance' along with 'participation', 'democracy' and 'rights' evokes a set of meanings different from those evoked when we talk about 'governance' and 'property rights', or 'governance' and 'corruption'.

Governance: for the Market or for Human Development?

The origin of governance explained in the previous section has exerted a fair amount of influence on the contents and approach of the governance agenda. Even when the IFI became aware of the importance of 'getting politics right', and not only 'getting prices right', they were not permitted by their mandates to intervene in the internal political affairs of their 'clients'. In this context, the governance agenda acted as a subterfuge to do so. For that reason, governance was presented like something merely technical. Therefore, the first generation of governance reforms sounds purely technocratic, and it is especially market-oriented. The most important features of good governance are protecting private property and reforming the judiciary in order to enforce contracts. Additionally, the fight against corruption and an effective bureaucracy are also relevant features in the discourse and practice of governance in IFI. Having protective legislation and honest officials will create a better climate for foreign investment, one of the spurs of growth that is regarded as the main development driver if not a synonym of it.

In sum, this 'official approach' sees good governance as a prerequisite for market institutions to be sound, which in turn, will prompt the economic growth that is said to pull people out of poverty.

However, and of particular relevance for us, is the fact that separate from this technocratic and market-oriented approach to governance, an alternative governance agenda has emerged from civil society organisations and some UN agencies, stressing the importance of good governance for excluded groups and poor people. 'Good governance' here tends to be a synonym for 'democratic governance'. The focus of this approach is no longer the market or economic growth, but human development. Among its fundamentals are voice, participation and empowerment of excluded groups, and accountability to them from state and private institutions.

These elements have a twofold importance. On the one hand, if we understand development as the process of enlargement of human capacities and freedoms, voice and participation are relevant in their own right, as included in the definition of development. They are ends, goods in themselves. Democratic governance has an intrinsic value for human development, because of the intrinsic value social and political participation have for human well-being. People who are not allowed to participate bear a capital privation.

On the other hand, those elements are means by which poor

people can reclaim better services or different policies to benefit them. That is to say, they are tools that contribute to strengthening the position of the poor in order to demand policies that enlarge their capacities, be it as workers, consumers, service receivers or citizens. This is an instrumental value in democratic governance. It allows citizens to voice their demands before the decision-makers, so that the latter can provide a consistent response to the former's needs.

Those questions are leading us to what probably is the core issue of governance problems: the power distribution in societies. The social distribution of power is reflected in formal institutions as much as in informal ones. Voice and accountability mechanisms and institutions cannot on their own shift the balance of power. An exclusive focus on those mechanisms might make us forget about the unequal and assymetric power relations within a society. That underlying reality may well erode all the effort devoted to improve democratic institutions.

Although at policy level, the human development approach to governance tends to focus on formal institutions (parliamentary and electoral programmes, access to justice initiatives, capacity building of local authorities …), it has helped raise the question of political power as a core issue of governance. In fact, it has provided a space for concepts such as citizenship, rights and empowerment. Through them, the governance agenda is moving from a technocratic approach to a political approach to development and poverty reduction. This move is not even or undisputed. The fight over the meaning of the concepts and the scope they adopt reaches also the idea of 'rights' and 'empowerment'. Ultimately, an often neglected dimension of poverty is its production. The groups and political processes involved in that production have to do with the 'rules of the game'. That is exactly what governance is.

This alternative approach has reminded us of the real nature of governance issues: governance is about power distribution, and not only about technical solutions. Since political processes and power relations are deeply rooted in the specific contexts, a 'one size-fits-all' approach to them and to institutions in which they crystallise is doomed to failure. However, the acknowledgement of the particularities in each country doesn't mean that we don't take into account the global processes that impinge on domestic governance problems. This is one of the characteristics of the alternative agenda of governance that is usually downplayed by the official one. When we look for the sources of bad or poor governance, the emphasis is placed on state institutions, culture, people and society. Logically, the IFI usually don't notice that big corporations, rich countries and international institutions they control are themselves part of the problem of poor governance, because of the policies they implement. As is said in the case of corruption, it is like a *tango*: it takes two to dance it.

A governance agenda that takes into account the excluded groups must address its political dimension and the issue of power distribution imbalance. In addition, it must be aware of the connection between local realities and global political and economic processes. The latter can reinforce the patterns of exclusion, but they can also bring opportunities for the excluded groups to face local constraints in the form of corrupt national governments, elite-controlled institutions, or anti-poor bias in legislation, to mention just a few.

Governance, in sum, is about the formation of policies and how the different stakeholders can, or cannot, engage in that process and influence it or not. The focal point of an alternative approach to governance is how the political capacities of the poor can grow stronger. If they have to compete and negotiate with elite groups, they need to be well equipped for that purpose. Political capacities of the poor refer to the institutional and organisational resources – including collective ideas – they have available for effective political action (Whitehead and Gray-Molina, in Houtzager and Moore, 2003). By way of political action they are able to put poverty issues on the agenda of the country. A very relevant dimension of poverty is the lack of resources for getting involved in politics (time, money, education, ideas, connections). On the one hand is an autonomous organisation, with the ability to table its own political initiatives. That means not being dependent ideologically on the definitions and proposals of others. On the other hand, is the possibility of building coalitions with other groups which do not necessarily represent the poor, in order to promote pro-poor policies. We honestly believe that the best work NGOs could do and are doing has to do with this. Dozens of church initiatives all over the world are also highlighting these points.

Populorum Progressio and the
Alternative Approach to Governance in Development

If we had to draw the most prominent features of the alternative approach to governance in development from the previous section, we would say that they are three: (i) a wider concept of development that embraces other dimensions apart from the economic one; (ii) among those dimensions, particularly relevant is the political one, that underscores the importance of participation of citizens – especially the excluded groups – in shaping the policies that affect them; and (iii) the attention that it pays not only to domestic factors and drivers of poor governance but to international ones as well.

Important traces of those three features are present in *Populorum Progressio*, albeit in a seminal way, or in the vocabulary of the time when it was written. Of course, we don't mean to compare discourses and ideas that are peculiar to different realms of human knowledge and experience. It would be naïve and a completely flawed approach to collate a church's analysis and those deriving from development studies. They aim at different objectives. They have different assumptions, sources, points of departure, methodologies. We cannot read an encyclical or another document of the church the same way as we read the latest Human Development Report or a paper from a scholar. We probably look at both with different questions in mind.

Nonetheless, from *Populorum Progressio*, as from other Catholic social teaching documents, stem some principles and values that, if not directly applicable when designing policies, can shed light and inform our analysis and ideas for action. Through the mediation of social sciences and the intervention of politics, they must be living values and principles in practice.

Which are those principles that lead us to conclude that they are supportive of an alternative agenda for governance in development? I will mention three:

The first is clearly enunciated in *Populorum Progressio*, n. 14: 'the development we speak of here cannot be restricted to economic growth alone. To be authentic, it must be rounded; it must foster the development of each man and of the whole man'. (We would say today in a more inclusive language 'of each human being and the whole human being'.) And it insists in n. 20 that authentic development is the 'transition from less human conditions to truly human ones'. For that to happen, economic growth does not suffice. Even worse, if economic mechanisms are left to operate on their own, and 'the existing machinery' is not modified, 'the disparity between rich and poor nations will increase rather than diminish' (n. 8).

The second is that among the other dimensions of this new concept of development, the political dimension now widely understood emerges as relevant in some expressions of *Populorum Progressio*, when it mentions that people are 'striving to exercise greater personal responsibility', for example, and the importance of acquiring 'social structures and processes (…) if their citizens are to achieve personal growth' (n. 6). Similarly, we now talk about the less human conditions – that is, underdevelopment – *Populorum Progressio* explicitly refers to 'oppressive political structures resulting from the abuse of ownership or the improper exercise of power' (n. 21). This is why economic deprivation is not regarded as the only source of inequality, but lack of power, initiative and responsibility ('agency' we would say in development jargon) is also critical in hampering a fully human development. That is how n. 9 expresses it: 'Then there are the flagrant inequalities not merely in the enjoyment of possessions, but even more in the exercise of power (…) in certain regions a privileged minority enjoys the refinements of life, while the rest of the inhabitants, impoverished and disunited, are deprived of almost all possibility of acting on their own initiative and responsibility'.

The third and final question addresses the issue of international cooperation and solidarity with developing countries, that is considered as a 'very important duty of the advanced nations' (n. 48), and without which no development of the individual is possible (n. 43). In order for it to be genuine cooperation, impositions must be avoided. The international solidarity must be based on dialogue, not on conditions, because 'a dialogue between those who contribute aid and those who receive it will permit a well-balanced assessment of the support to be provided (…) taking into account the real needs of the receiving countries' (n. 54).

The final objective of cooperation is not an increased influence or domination of rich countries over poor ones, but rather that each nation becomes owner and shaper of its own decisions in an atmosphere of international relations characterised by respect. True international cooperation 'should allow all peoples to become the artisans of their destiny' (n. 65). This goes against the trend of trying to transfer or impose models that are not rooted in democratically-exerted choices.

References

Cornwall, Andrea and Karen Brock (2005) *What do Buzzwords do for Development Policy? A critical look at 'Poverty Reduction', 'Participation' and 'Empowerment'*. Geneva: UNRISD.

Fukuyama, Francis (2004) *State-building. Governance and World Order in the 21st Century*. Cornell University Press, New York.

Graña, François (2005) *Diálogo social y gobernanza en la era del 'Estado mínimo'*, (Papeles de la Oficina Técnica, 16), Montevideo: Cinterfor/OIT.

Houtzager, Peter and Mick Moore, M. (eds) (2003) *Changing Paths: International Development and the New Politics of Inclusion*, University of Michigan.

Rodrik, Dani (1999) *Institutions for High-Quality Growth: What they are and how to acquire them*. International Monetary Fund Conference on Second-Generation Reforms. Washington DC.

Sen, Amartya (2000) *Desarrollo y libertad. Editorial Planeta* (English title: *Development as freedom*).

Notes
1. Only in the second part of 2006, three important governance-related documents were produced by key donors. The World Bank approved its new strategy on 'Governance and Anticorruption' (September 2006). The European Commission published a communication on 'Governance in the New European Consensus for Development' (August 2006). The United Kingdom named its new white paper on development 'Make Governance Work for the Poor' (July 2006).

2. For instance, the *World Development Report 1997* addresses the issue of the State and Development. No position is taken regarding the desirability of democracy, since no clear link is found between democracy and development outcomes. Just four years later, the *World Development Report 2000/01* declares that democracy is intrinsically valuable for human wellbeing, and a good in its own right.

Unequal Power Relations and the Denial of Opportunities: A South Asian Reading of Populorum Progressio

Prakash Louis SJ

Global Development Efforts

In September 2000, the world's leaders adopted the UN Millennium Declaration, committing their nations to stronger global efforts to reduce poverty, improve health and promote peace, human rights and environmental sustainability (UNDP, 2003). This Millennium Declaration adopted at the Millennium Summit reflects the concerns of 147 heads of state and governments. The Declaration focused on the following areas: (i) values and principles, (ii) peace, security and harmony, (iii) development and poverty eradication, (iv) protecting our common environment, (v) human rights, democracy and good governance, (vi) protecting the vulnerable, (vii) meeting the specific needs of Africa, (viii) strengthening the United Nations (UN, 2000).

Significantly the entire exercise was undertaken to set targets or goals that were measurable. In the Millennium Declaration, it was stated that 'We request the General Assembly to review on a regular basis the progress made in implementing the provisions of this Declaration, and ask the Secretary-General to issue periodic reports for consideration by the General Assembly and as a basis for further action.' Thus, those who were involved in the formulation of the Millennium Development Goals were already aware of the need to include systems for assessment and to facilitate further action plans.

As part of the awareness and implementation of the Millennium Development Goals in South Asia many activities, events, programmes and campaigns were undertaken. Campaigns like *Wada na todo*, that is, 'Fulfil Your Promises' and the Global Campaign against Poverty were initiated by the national, regional and global civil society organisations to ensure that governments act on their policy commitments made both at the national and international levels. These efforts resulted in the summit, 'Stand Up against Poverty' on 15 and 16 October 2006. The Global Day of Action against Poverty was also organised for 17 October 2006. Yet, despite these efforts poverty and hunger continue unabated. Moreover, they have a debilitating effect on those social groups and nations that are already discriminated against and marginalised.

One of the fundamental questions facing the global family today is, despite the huge progress of civilisation, why are the vast majority of social groups and nations untouched by development or the outcome of development? Despite innumerable and continuous local, national, regional and global efforts to eradicate poverty and lead people on the path of development, why are many people still in the iron grip of poverty, hunger and misery? Do people really count in the process and outcome of development, or are they there to service the development of those who have the power to underdevelop people for their own gain?

Pope Paul VI, as far back as the 1960s, had some deep insights into the crisis of development and insisted on the development of people. In *Populorum Progressio* he argued: 'The development of people has the church's close attention, particularly the development of those peoples who are striving to escape from hunger, misery, endemic diseases and ignorance; of those who are looking for a wider share in the benefits of civilisation and a more active improvement of their human qualities; of those who are aiming purposefully at their complete fulfilment ... (n. 1). 'Today the people in hunger are making a dramatic appeal to the peoples blessed with abundance. The church shudders at this cry of anguish and calls each one to give a loving response of charity to this brother's cry for help' (n. 3).

On the fortieth anniversary of the publication of *Populorum Progressio* it is expedient to revisit this encyclical and draw inspiration for the Christian social commitment to address the unequal power relations and denial of equal opportunity. This chapter presents a South Asian reading of *Populorum Progressio*.

Locating *Populorum Progressio*

During his leadership as the universal pastor, Paul VI expected and urged the universal church and its episcopal bodies to become a loving and serving church. The following initiatives highlight this fact: (i) Three synods held in 1969, 1971 and 1974 deal with issues that are related to human development, well-being and dignity; (ii) his address to the national and regional conferences of bishops encouraged and directed them to give the poor and the oppressed a central place in their pastoral concerns; (iii) following from these, he established the Pontifical Commission for Justice and Peace. This commission became the agent through which the church intervenes in justice and peace issues both within the church and in the world.

Two interlinked themes are central to the encyclical *Populorum Progressio*. The first one is 'the human person's complete development' and the second is 'the development of the human race in the spirit of solidarity'. In his interaction with various social groups and religious communities, and during his travels to various regions of the world, Paul VI seems to have been affected by poverty and hunger that he witnessed. But above all, he seems to have been concerned by growing injustice. These experiences led him to state in bold terms, 'There is also the scandal of glaring inequalities not merely in the employment of possessions but even in the exercise of power' (n. 9).

Thus, Paul VI tries to highlight and address two interrelated aspects of development and underdevelopment – power and powerlessness – in this encyclical. He argues that while the vast masses are denied the fruits of development, a small minority continues to benefit from it. However, it is not just the appropriation of wealth and resources, but also unequal power relations that must be addressed by the church.

Furthermore, a careful reader of *Populorum Progressio* will realise that the encyclical points towards the structural nature of poverty and misery as well as the structural dynamics of power and powerlessness, and the encyclical does not stop there. It goes on to present a fuller vision of human development and of the development of all human beings.

Development and Underdevelopment

In the South Asian region, development, by definition and conceptually, denoted progress – social, economic, educational, cultural, scientific and technological – brought about by planned/programmed efforts to inaugurate an era of orderly and peaceful transformation of a society towards constitutionality. An attempt was made to interface between private and public sectors to ensure a mixed economy, but public enterprises dominated the economic sphere while the private enterprises were comparatively limited. Moreover, with nation-building at the top of the agenda, ensuring people's participation and promoting community development was of vital importance.

A mapping of the extensive literature on development points to the following conceptions of development: (i) Development is usually seen as economic growth. Economic indicators are used to measure the growth or stagnation of the economy of a country. (ii) Development is related to improvement in life chances. Many of the development agencies refer to efforts to provide for the basic needs of people, i.e. improved facilities in education, health, housing, and social welfare. (iii) There are others who would consider development as growth and redistribution. Here development is equated with growth, equity and self-reliance. (iv) Finally, development is increasingly seen as a process of liberation from dependency and exploitation.

To further unravel and explore the multifaceted realities of development, one needs to dovetail economic growth with social security and equality. Development now is not just related to technology, neither is it solely dependent upon human endeavour. It is intimately related to the extent of a group's control over resources, both human and material. It inevitably includes the process of inclusion of some and the exclusion of other groups. The overtly glittering and glamorous process, paradigm and outcome of development obscured the unequal and iniquitous socioeconomic structure of India. While the skewed social structure determined the process and outcome of development, development in turn also reinforced a skewed sociopolitical and economic structure.

The historical fact that affluence and destitution, conspicuous consumption and continued starvation have become two sides of the same national and international process of centralised command over natural resources is of seminal significance. The irony is that those who are engaged in production in the most difficult and arduous conditions are forced to starve while those who are engaged in consumption continue to control the means of production. This divide has been accepted as fixed and final, ironically, in an age that swears by equity and justice and claims to be committed to eradication of all forms of disabilities that humans have created for themselves through the ages.

Thus, it is dawning on all those who want to understand the various dimensions of local and international development that development is not a neutral entity. Underdevelopment of a vast majority of people and countries is directly related to the unprecedented development of some people and countries. Individuals, social groups and countries who wield power also control the economic sphere. Thus, with even the best of the intentions, goals and targets set for eradicating poverty and ensuring human development and dignity seem to be at the best public pronouncements. Table 1 highlights this fact very clearly. (*Human Development Report 2001*, Oxford University Press: New Delhi, p. 22.)

Table 1: A Balance Sheet of Human Development

GOALS	ACHIEVEMENTS	UNFINISHED PATH
Halve the proportion of people living in extreme poverty.	Between 1990 and 1998 the proportion of people living on less than $1 (1993 PPP US$) a day in developing countries was reduced from 29% to 24%.	Even if the proportion is halved by 2015, there will still be 900 million people living in extreme poverty in the developing world.
Halve the proportion of people suffering from hunger.	The number of undernourished people in the developing world fell by 40 million between 1990-92 and 1996-98.	The developing world still has 826 million undernourished people.
Halve the proportion of people without access to safe water.	Around 80% of people in the developing world now have access to improved water sources.	Nearly one billion people still lack access to improved water sources.

GOALS	ACHIEVEMENTS	UNFINISHED PATH
Enrol all children in primary school. Achieve universal completion of primary schooling.	By 1997 more than 70 countries had primary net enrolment ratios over 80%. In 29 of the 46 countries with data, 80% of children enrolled reach grade 5.	In the next 15 years provision must be made for the 113 million children now out of primary school and the million more who will enter the school-age population.
Empower women and eliminate gender disparities in primary and secondary education.	By 1997 the female enrolment ratio in developing countries had reached 89% of the male ratio at the primary level and 82% at the secondary level.	In 20 countries girls' secondary enrolment ratios are still less than two-third of boys' enrolment ratios.
Reduce maternal mortality ratios by three-quarters.	Only 32 countries have achieved a reported maternal mortality ratio of less than 20 per 100,000 live births.	In 21 countries the reported maternal mortality ratio exceeds 500 per 100,000 live births.
Reduce infant mortality rates by two-thirds.* Reduce under-five mortality rates by two-thirds.	In 1990-99 infant mortality was reduced by more than 10%, from 64 per 1,000 live births to 56. Under-five mortality was reduced from 93 per 1,000 live births to 80 in 1990-99.	Sub-Saharan Africa has an infant mortality rate of more than 100 and an under-five mortality rate of more than 170 – and has been making slower progress than other regions.
Halt and begin to reverse the spread of HIV/AIDS.	In a few countries, such as Uganda and possibly Zambia, HIV/AIDS prevalence is showing signs of decline.	Around 36 million people are living with HIV/AIDS.
Provide access for all who want reproductive health services.*	Contraceptive prevalence has reached nearly 50% in developing countries.	Around 120 million couples who want to use contraception do not have access to it.
Implement national strategies for sustainable development by 2005 to reverse the loss of environmental resources by 2015.*	The number of countries adopting sustainable development strategies rose from fewer than 25 in 1990 to more than 50 in 1997.	Implementation of the strategies remains minimal.

*International development goal.

In the global arena, the gap between the rich and poor people and countries is increasing. The UN Conference on Trade and Development's (UNCTAD) 1999 annual report has examined the issues of the growing worldwide gap between the rich and poor as a result of globalisation. Some of its revelations are:

- Since 1994, the 200 richest people in the world have more than doubled their net worth to one trillion dollars.
- Industrialised countries of Europe and the US hold 97 per cent of all patents worldwide.
- The income gap between the richest fifth of the world's people and the poorest fifth increased from 30 to 1 in 1960 to 74 to 1 in 1997.
- Tanzania's debt payment is nine times what it spends on primary health care and four times what it spends on primary education.
- The value of the illegal drug trade was estimated at 400 billion dollars in 1995, about 8 per cent of world trade.
- In the US in 1960 a chief executive officer of a company earned on average an income that was 40 times the average income of a factory worker. In 1993 it was 149 times more.
- Among more than 600 professionals in the World Bank, the ratio of economists to social scientists is 28 to 1. These economists, with no hold on ground reality, and with no loyalty to their own country or society, determine the destiny of more than 75 developing countries.

The South Asian Scenario
It has become a trend in an 'underdeveloped' country like India that a small segment of the population continues to thrive on the unequal distribution of resources as well as unequal access to the developmental processes. On the other hand, the state is slowly and steadily abdicating its social responsibilities towards the vulnerable communities.

One of the Millennium Development Goals is stated as: 'Eradicate extreme poverty and hunger' (Goal 1). Along with this goal two targets were set by the international community. Target 1: Halve, between 1990 and 2015, the proportion of people whose income is less than $1 a day. Target 2: Halve between

1990 and 2015, the proportion of people who suffer from hunger. These goals and targets in themselves sound most appropriate and practical. The reality seems to be different, however.

At the national level in India, for the last 50 years there have been planned attempts to eradicate poverty. One can count over 100 schemes that were envisaged to eradicate poverty over the years. The reality, however, is that more than 34.7 per cent of the population is still forced to live below the poverty line. This number goes up to 79.3 per cent if one calculates the level of poverty at $2 a day. However, if one examines the level of poverty among the weaker sections or the marginalised population then the picture is more alarming. Over 56 per cent of the Scheduled Castes or the lower castes and 54 per cent of the Scheduled Tribes/Indigenous Peoples are still living below the poverty line. While the small and marginal farmers are forced to commit suicide the agricultural labourers are succumbing to starvation deaths.

Most of the South Asian countries experimented with 'planned economy' in the last five decades. They even introduced land reform policies hoping that this would lead to production and equal distribution, but the results were far from satisfactory. Keeping in line with liberalisation and privatisation pressure, most of these countries also enacted a 'New Economic Policy'. It was stated that this would lift the descending economy to newer levels of growth. The reality, however, is that while the economy grows poverty remains and the number of poor people is on the increase.

Table 2 (overleaf) highlights the fact that in most of the South Asian countries more than one third of the population is forced to live below the poverty line. Sri Lanka and Pakistan seem to have fared even better than China, but one cannot compare these countries with South Africa and the United States. Furthermore, the health and educational indicators emphasise that the scenario for South Asia is grim. Countries like India are supposed to be at the forefront of IT revolution but as regards aspects of life affecting the ordinary masses India is way behind and is ranked 127 in the Human Development Index.

Table 2: Human Development Indexes of South Asian and other countries

Countries	Pop. Living below 1$ a day %	IMR – per 1000 births	MMR – per 1000 births	Tuberculosis cases per 100,000	Rural Pop. with drinking water %	Urban Pop. with sanitation %	Adult literacy %	HDI ranking
Bangladesh	36.0	51	600	211	97.0	71.0	40.6	139
India	34.7	67	440	199	79.0	61.0	58.0	127
Nepal	37.7	66	830	135	87.0	73.0	42.9	143
Pakistan	13.4	84	200	178	87.0	95.0	44.0	144
Sri Lanka	6.6	17	60	50	70.0	95.0	91.9	99
China	16.1	31	60	39	66.0	69.0	85.8	104
S. Africa	2.0	56	340	237	73.0	93.0	85.6	111
US	-	7	12	2	100.0	100.0	100.0	7

Source: *Human Development Report 2003*, New Delhi: Oxford University Press, 2003

Interestingly, since development is invariably discussed in economic terms the real impact of development continues to be seen in statistical terms. In the recent past there has been a growing awareness that any debate on development has to pay attention to the entire sociopolitical, economic and cultural aspects in its totality. From this perspective one can state that development involves ensuring that the benefits of development are extended to all the segments of the population and in a particular way to the most downtrodden of any society or country.

Rereading *Populorum Progressio*

Paul VI mentioned in unambiguous terms that development has to be integral and that it should be linked to the notion that the rights and dignity of human beings must not be denied. According to *Populorum Progressio*, 'Development cannot be limited to mere economic growth. In order to be authentic, it must be rounded; it must be complete, that is, integral' (n. 14). One of the fundamental tasks of those actively involved in international economic matters is to achieve for all people a form of development that is integral, that is to say, the development in question must 'promote the good of every person and the whole person' (n. 14). These insights have guided various interventions of the church in these matters.

Over the years, many international organisations and forums have highlighted similar concerns. The Social Development Summit at Copenhagen in 1995 crystallised the world debate on social development, with the participant governments agreeing to accord social development and human wellbeing the highest priority both now and into the 21st century. The framework for action that evolved there included:

   (i) Place people at the centre of development, and economy at the service of human needs;

   (ii) Integrate economic and social policies to make them mutually supportive;

   (iii) Recognise that sound and broad-based economic policies are a necessary foundation to achieve sustained social development;

   (iv) Promote a more just distribution of income and access to resources through equity and equality of opportunity for people at all levels;

(v) Recognise that empowering people to strengthen their own capacities is the main objective of development and its principal resource.

The World Social Forum's Charter of Principles has the following alternatives to a monistic, unilinear and hegemonic economic development: (i) The alternatives proposed at the World Social Forum stand in opposition to a process of capitalist globalisation led by the large multinational corporations and by the governments and international institutions at the service of those corporations' interests. They are designed to ensure that globalisation in solidarity will prevail as a new stage in world history. This will respect universal human rights and those of all citizens – men and women – of all nations and environments and will depend on democratic international systems and institutions at the service of social justice, equality and the sovereignty of peoples. (ii) As a context for interrelations, the World Social Forum seeks to strengthen and create new national and international links among organisations and movements of civil society, that – in both public and private life – will increase the capacity for social resistance to the process of dehumanisation the world is undergoing and reinforce the humanising measures being taken by these movements and organisations.

Historical data bear testimony to the fact that the church at different times made profound statements about some of the crucial aspects of development and human beings. *Populorum Progressio* stated: 'Following on the Second Vatican Ecumenical Council a renewed consciousness of the demands of the gospel makes it her duty to put herself at the service of all, to help them grasp their serious problem in all its dimensions, and to convince them that solidarity in action at this turning point in human history is a matter of urgency' (n. 1). While these kinds of public pronouncements have constituted the social teachings of the church, it has not made serious and systematic attempts to examine its own ideology and its operations with regard to development. The basic questions that the church needs to raise at this juncture are: how does it view the ever-increasing dehumanisation of masses all over the globe? In an unequal social order, what is the contribution of its own welfare and developmental activities? Does its theology and spirituality respond to the poverty, misery and inhuman conditions to which the masses are subjected by development?

Today human existence itself is threatened by dehumanising cultures. There is the culture of death that enforces starvation death, suicide, abortion, female infanticide, murders of politically-conscious people who oppose the existing unjust socio-economic structures, the slow 'murder' of the underprivileged who are denied food and basic facilities. There is the culture of poverty, which has forced the masses into malnutrition, hunger and slow death, despite the fact that it is they who toil to produce food and other products. There is the culture of domination and subjugation, which contradicts every form of freedom and liberty. And there is the culture of silence, which forces the oppressed to suffer silently every form of inhuman treatment and finally reduces them to subhuman living. It is with this backdrop that the church has to be proactive to make development work for the common masses all over the globe. Will the church learn from its own traditions? This is the question that the rereading of *Populorum Progressio* raises even four decades after its promulgation.

References

Compendium of the Social Doctrine of the Church (2004), Pontifical Council for Justice and Peace, Pauline Publications.

Desrochers, John (1982) *The Social Teaching of the Church*, Bangalore: John Desrochers

Sharma, K. L. (1986) *Development: Socio-cultural Dimensions*, Jaipur: Rawat Publications.

UN (2000) *United Nations Millennium Declaration*, New York: United Nations Department of Public Information.

UNCTAD (1999) *Annual Report.* UN Conference on Trade and Development.

UN (2003) Millennium Development Goals, *Human Development Report 2003*, New Delhi: Oxford University Press.

Populorum Progressio
in the Era of Globalisation

Peadar Kirby

When *Populorum Progressio* was issued in 1967, the term 'globalisation' had not yet been coined, much less come to assume the central role in interpreting the nature of the international system that it now plays. Yet, in announcing in its opening paragraphs that 'the social question has become worldwide' (n. 3), Pope Paul VI anticipated what is perhaps the greatest challenge that faces today's globalised world. Furthermore, reading the encyclical in the light of that challenge shows that, while some of the central themes developed by Pope Paul have now become key elements of today's development politics, the more fundamental critiques contained in *Populorum Progressio* are probably even more relevant today than they were 40 years ago and certainly are further from being addressed in the realm of practical global politics. To this extent, *Populorum Progressio* stands as a searing indictment of our globalised economic and social order and offers insights into what needs to be done that urgently require to be seen and acted upon.

This chapter begins by identifying what has been achieved in the past 40 years of development efforts that might gladden the heart of Pope Paul. It then goes on to argue that the central moral and social critique contained in *Populorum Progressio* is in fact even more neglected in today's world than when the encyclical was written, and to develop what this critique has to offer to analysis of, and action on, the sort of globalisation that is now dominant. The chapter's final section adopts a more personal tone in describing how, in my young adulthood, *Populorum Progressio* exercised a profound influence on my own critical capacities, an influence that has endured over the intervening decades and has been confirmed and reinforced as I have, through study, travel and teaching, extended and deepened my own knowledge of the nature of the global system and how it operates.

Achievements

Populorum Progressio is organised around two themes. The first offers a rich vision of the human person and of people's aspirations (n. 6), and Pope Paul makes clear that what the church offers is 'a global vision' of the person and of the human race (n. 13). This could be called the encyclical's qualitative dimension and it provides the basis for the radical critique of the global order that suffuses the whole document. The second theme is the more quantitative one, as the Pope emphasises that all people in the world have a right to realise their aspirations to a more complete self-fulfilment. While such an ambitious approach towards the topic of international development was novel when the encyclical was issued, a focus on people's ability to realise their own aspirations lies at the heart of the human development approach pioneered by the United Nations Development Programme (UNDP) in its annual *Human Development Report*, first published in 1990. The UNDP defines human development as a process of enlarging people's choices to lead a long and healthy life, to acquire knowledge, to have access to the resources needed for a decent standard of living while preserving it for future generations, ensuring human security and achieving equality for all women and men. This is now the mainstream concept of development worldwide, and summarises well all the dimensions of a Christian vision of development as outlined by Pope Paul in *Populorum Progressio* (n. 14). Of all the changes in the arena of international development that have taken place since 1967, this would probably most gladden his heart.

But other practical reforms for which he called have also been realised. For example, the Pope was very concerned about equity in trade negotiations and stressed that there cannot be different standards for developed and developing countries (n. 61). While he recognised that real equality of opportunity between both groups of countries 'is a long-term objective', he urged that 'to reach it we must begin now to create true equality in discussions and negotiations', and suggested that 'international agreements on a rather wide scale would be helpful' (n. 61). This is precisely what the World Trade Organisation (WTO), established in 1995, seeks to provide, perhaps even beyond what Pope Paul might have thought possible. However, whether the WTO is actually helping to 'establish general norms for regulating certain prices, for guaranteeing certain types of production, for supporting certain new industries', as Pope Paul seemed to presume would be the outcome of international agreements, is of course open to serious question.

In relation to aid, recent years have also given grounds for hope, reversing the decline that was evident in the 1990s. Most developed countries have now given commitments either to reach the UN's long-standing target of 0.7 per cent of GNP in international aid by a certain date, or at least to advance towards a definite percentage of it. This goes some way towards meeting the strong call of Pope Paul to rich countries to share their superfluous wealth. As he warned: 'Otherwise their continued greed will certainly call down upon them the judgement of God and the wrath of the poor, with consequences no one can foretell' (n. 49). Furthermore, these efforts are not isolated or scattered but are done as part of a concerted planning effort, exactly what the Pope called for.

Finally, there are other elements of *Populorum Progressio* that form part of today's mainstream development agenda in a way that they did not in 1967. Among these is the importance of investment in basic education and a continuing decline in illiteracy in most parts of the world (n. 35), a dialogue to help developing countries being overwhelmed by debts (n. 54), addressing the problem of population growth (n. 37) and, through the UN Secretary General's Global Compact, an effort to ensure that private companies, particularly multinational corporations, sign up to a basic set of social and environmental standards, echoing Pope Paul's concerns that industrialists be the 'initiators of social progress and human advancement' (n. 70). Identifying these ways in which some of the themes of the encyclical are finding implementation serves not only to underline the far-seeing vision of Pope Paul but also suggests ways in which his document has made a practical impact. However, as is all too obvious from even a cursory knowledge of today's globalised world, the gulf between the developed and developing countries remains very wide, with at least 1.3 billion people living on less than $1 a day, and with the gap between the incomes of the top fifth of income earners and the bottom fifth growing at an alarming rate. Pope Paul would hardly be satisfied were he still alive to witness just how meagre have been the results of the intervening 40 years of development efforts.

'The Woeful System'

Investigating why the urgent ambition announced by Pope Paul in 1967 to 'bring about a world that is more human towards all ... where all will be able to give and receive, without one group making progress at the expense of the other' (n. 44) has not been realised (and in many ways is even further from realisation) requires that we analyse how globalisation has affected the prospects for development. In doing this, it is necessary to bear in mind some of the central analytical tools employed by Pope Paul, which offer something that is all too often missing from today's concentration on global flows of trade, capital and information. For the Pope begins from the understanding that our world is riven by 'glaring inequalities not merely in the enjoyment of possessions *but even more* in the exercise of power' (n. 9; emphasis added). This, of course, is the fundamental structural feature of our world that profoundly shapes the intensified flows of trade, capital and information that characterise globalisation, and therefore the developmental impact they can have. It is in writing about free trade that the Pope applies this insight most clearly, where he recognises that free trade is advantageous 'when the parties involved are not affected by any excessive inequalities of economic power'; but 'the situation is no longer the same when economic conditions differ too widely from country to country' with the result that 'prices which are "freely" set in the market can produce unfair results' (n. 58).

This criticism is based on recognition of the fundamental structural inequality of today's global order and, interestingly, draws on and applies to the situation of international relations, an insight from Pope Leo XIII's encyclical *Rerum Novarum* of 1892 on the inequalities between employer and worker in the labour market. Applied to the nature of the global order, it provides the basis for understanding why 'modern economics [l]eft to itself works rather to widen the differences in the world's level of life, not to diminish them: rich peoples enjoy rapid growth whereas the poor develop slowly' (n. 8). This critique applies much more forcefully to our globalised world (in other words, it uncovers a far more central dynamic shaping today's world) than it did to the world of more protected economies in which *Populorum Progressio* was written.

This brings the Pope to criticise liberal capitalism in very sharp terms: it is the 'woeful system' referred to in the title of this section. His words are important enough to quote at some length:

> But it is unfortunate that on these new conditions of society [the Pope is here referring to industrialisation, entrepreneurship and what he calls 'research and discovery', the subjects of the previous paragraph] a system has been constructed which considers profit as the key motive for economic progress, competition as the supreme law of economics, and private ownership of the means of production as an absolute right that has no limits and carries no corresponding social obligation. This unchecked liberalism leads to dictatorship rightly denounced by Pius XI as producing 'the international imperialism of money'. One cannot condemn such abuses too strongly by solemnly recalling once again that the economy is at the service of man. (n. 26)

If in the 1960s, which was the high point of managed economies, whether of the social market variety or of the socialist variety, such a critique could be taken as applying to only a small number of countries and to some extreme voices within economics, the advent of globalisation and the emergence of a single global economy has changed all that. For, under the rubric of neoliberalism, since the early 1990s the nature of the global economy has dramatically changed and countries' developmental prospects depend on their ability to survive in a situation of ever more intense and ruthless competition, imposed by global organisations such as the World Trade Organisation, the World Bank and the International Monetary Fund (see Harvey, 2005, for a good history of this change).

This critique of 'a type of capitalism [that] has been the source of excessive suffering, injustices and fratricidal conflicts whose effects still persist' (n. 26) highlights the continuing vital importance of *Populorum Progressio* for our globalised world. Indeed, in many ways it is even more important today as such a critique is far rarer in our world than it was 40 years ago and faces a much more hostile climate in which neoclassical economics has taken on a hegemonic position in the social sciences, in public discourse and in practical politics. Neither can it be underestimated how central it is to the thinking of Pope Paul: again and again he returns to it. '[T]he mere free play of competition could never assure successful development', he writes in paragraph 33 and 'too often creates an economic dictatorship' (n. 59). In critiquing free trade, he adds that 'it is the fundamental principle of "liberalism", as the rule for commercial exchange, which is questioned here' (n. 58).

Among the most original insights of the encyclical and one that is extremely pertinent to the situation of our world are the Pope's comments on economic growth. Widely seen as an absolute good providing the justification for economic liberalisation and the weakening of social and environmental regulations, Pope Paul instead writes that 'all growth is ambivalent', being essential if the human person is to develop, but also imprisoning if it is considered to be the supreme good (n. 19). This again puts him at variance with economic liberalism. And in a paragraph that is worth quoting, as it applies with particular force to a country like Ireland that has lived through an economic boom, the Pope casts a critical eye on the consequences of liberal capitalism:

> But the acquiring of temporal goods can lead to greed, to the insatiable desire for more, and can make increased power a tempting objective. Individuals, families and nations can be overcome by avarice, be they poor or rich, and all can fall victim to a stifling materialism (n. 18).

The end result, both for nations and for individuals, is a 'form of moral underdevelopment' (n. 19). In this way, Pope Paul turns on its head the claim of liberal capitalism to lead to development – so often, even where it is successful, the result turns out to be a new form of underdevelopment that 'becomes an obstacle to individual fulfilment and to man's true greatness' (n. 19).

There are many practical insights and principles that flow from this central critique that have much to offer our understanding of today's globalisation as well as what needs to be done to make it more humane and developmental. An important one is Pope Paul's understanding of freedom. In marked contrast to today's dominant view that gives priority to the economic freedom of the individual – and reshapes society to offer as total a guarantee as possible to ensure this form of freedom – the Pope enunciates a more social and challenging view of freedom. In describing the objective of a world where everyone, regardless of race, religion or nationality, can live a fully human life, he adds that this would be a world 'where freedom is not an empty word and where the poor man Lazarus can sit down at the same table with the rich man'. This turns on its head the priorities of today's economic orthodoxy as it would require 'great generosity, much sacrifice and unceasing effort on the part of the rich man', including paying higher taxes so that public authorities can intensify their development efforts, higher prices for imported goods so that the producer could be more justly rewarded, and leaving one's country to assist in the development of young nations (n. 47).

In restating the core Catholic principle of the universal purpose of all created things, the Pope furthermore makes clear the limits of today's dominant economic freedom. The right to private property can never be exercised to the detriment of the common good, and this may sometimes demand the expropriation of landed property (n. 22 and 23) while, in a paragraph that is perhaps even more applicable in a world of tax havens and tax exiles, the Pope also states that 'it is unacceptable that citizens with abundant incomes from the resources and activity of their country should transfer a considerable part of this income abroad purely for their own advantage' (n. 24).

A fundamental principle that flows from the central critique of *Populorum Progressio* could not be more pertinent to today's world. This refers to the relation between state and market or, as Pope Paul more accurately puts it, between public authorities and the market. In contradistinction to those who argue that the state is inefficient, he emphasises the role of public authorities in setting the ends to be achieved and the means to achieve them, taking care to associate private initiative and intermediate bodies, thus preventing the danger of concentration of power and its arbitrary use (n. 33). Central to the tasks of these authorities is to keep the competitive market 'within the limits which make it just and moral, and therefore human' (n. 61). He makes clear that 'to speak of development is in effect to show as much concern for social progress as for economic growth' (n. 34) and urges 'an economy which is put at the service of man' (n. 86).

These proposals come close to the means used by the one group of developing countries that have succeeded in transforming their economies and societies, the East Asian Tigers (see Amsden, 2001). Anticipating by decades proposals that are today advanced to deal with the excesses of globalisation (see, for example, UNDP, 1999), Pope Paul proposed 'a worldwide authority capable of acting effectively on the juridical and political plane' (n. 78) and a 'great World Fund to be made up of part of the money spent on arms, to relieve the most destitute of this world' (n. 51). Neither of these has yet been realised despite the Pope's plea, in relation to the world fund: 'Would that those in authority listened to our words before it is too late' (n. 53). Again anticipating a central topic of today's globalisation, he recognised the 'conflict of civilisations' though not as today's version of a conflict between Christian and Islamic civilisations, but between industrial civilisation and the traditional civilisations that it tends to undermine (n. 10). In this situation, he urges a dialogue between civilisations, one based on an encounter of peoples and not just on commodities or technical skills (n. 73).

Towards the end of *Populorum Progressio*, Pope Paul shares the common experience of all radical reformers: 'whether some would consider such hopes too utopian' (n. 79). However, perhaps surprisingly, he responds that those who would claim this are not realistic enough as they do not realise 'the dynamism of a world that desires to live more fraternally'. He has also given enough warnings throughout the encyclical letter about the consequences of delaying the 'bold transformations, innovations that go deep' and 'urgent reforms' required (n. 32). Because of his fears that 'excessive economic, social and cultural inequalities among peoples … are a danger to peace' (n. 75), he coined what is perhaps the encyclical's best-known phrase: 'development is the new name for peace' (the title of Section 4 of Part II).

He wrote of the temptations to violence in this situation (n. 30) and of the wrath of the poor. Ultimately, he urges 'the duties of human solidarity' not only among those of us currently alive, but to the generations that come after us (again a far-seeing anticipation of the 1987 Brundtland Report on the environment and development that recognises our responsibilities to future generations).

One cannot come away from reading this encyclical without being struck by its passionate conviction and sense of urgency about the necessity for radical change in the unjust and inequitable structures of the global order. There is here the young radical's impatience for change, and little of the measured and balanced tones of the senior churchman. Yet, 40 years later we live in a more unjust and violent world, a world now threatened by forms of violence that could not be contemplated when the letter was written. Now we have a form of globalisation that is based on a return to the core tenets of liberal capitalism and in which the restraining hold of public policies has been greatly weakened (indeed, public policies are now reshaped to promote a social order based on liberal capitalism). In this situation, *Populorum Progressio* and its message of a deep and integral Christian humanism based on bonds of worldwide solidarity remains more important than when it was issued. Any hope of addressing effectively the worldwide nature of today's social question rests on taking its critique seriously and seeking to build a social order in conformity with it.

A Personal Debt
Rereading this encyclical letter has entailed something of a journey back to my past. For I see from my copy that I bought it on 27 October 1971, just as I was entering adulthood. Its importance to me is indicated by the fact that it is heavily underlined – with a fountain pen in black ink, with a red biro and with a yellow marker. Phrases are underlined, once and even twice, double lines against sentences and paragraphs highlight them, arrows point to sections and, in one place, question marks indicate some disagreement with the Pope's claim that colonialism brought some benefits to the colonised countries. It was a text to which I

obviously returned again and again in those formative years, finding there illuminating insights.

Only in returning decades later, do I realise that the central insights of this encyclical letter have marked my analysis of the world and my moral orientation towards it in profound and enduring ways. Indeed, I am amazed at how much some of the overriding priorities of my contemporary work (in research, writing and teaching) are rooted in this document – its critique of liberal capitalism, its identification of inequality in all its forms as perhaps the most fundamental ill of the world, its emphasis that the economy should be at the service of human beings, its recognition that development must give equal priority to the social as to the economic, its core insight that injustice is a structural feature of the global order, making some richer while others fall further behind, its view that economic growth is always ambivalent, its balancing of a material view of development with one emphasising the importance of culture and spirituality and, ultimately, its belief that radical change is urgent but is also possible. Its translation into English leaves a lot to be desired (and must put off some readers) and its constant use of 'man' to include all human beings jars on today's sensibilities, yet for Christians at least it must remain one of the great seminal social texts of the 20th century and is certainly as fresh, urgent and passionately relevant now as when promulgated.

References

Amsden, Alice H. (2002), *The Rise of the 'Rest': Challenges to the West from Late-Industrializing Economies*, New York: Oxford University Press.

Harvey, David (2005), *A Brief History of Neoliberalism*, Oxford: Oxford University Press.

UNDP (1999), *Human Development Report 1999*, New York: Oxford University Press.

Facing up to the Development Challenge of AIDS

Michael J Kelly SJ

Populorum Progressio was published more than 14 years before HIV and AIDS exploded on the world. But the language of the encyclical and many of its thoughts are as relevant to an AIDS-infected world as they were to the world of the 1960s. Thus, when it speaks of people's efforts to escape the ravages of hunger, poverty, endemic disease and ignorance, to remove every obstacle that offends human dignity, and to exercise greater personal responsibility, it is speaking a language that resonates well in today's world with HIV and AIDS.

Even more remarkable is the encyclical's call for the establishment of a world fund, financed by a levy on military expenditures, to relieve the needs of impoverished people and promote the work of national development (nn. 51-53). This was in 1967, decades before the United Nations took action to establish the Global Fund to Fight AIDS, Tuberculosis and Malaria. The Global Fund is replenished by voluntary contributions from developed countries, but room still exists for it to be enlarged by the kind of levy that Pope Paul envisaged. Military expenditures have greatly increased since his time, exceeding one trillion dollars in 2004, but the needs of impoverished and disease-affected countries have likewise grown immeasurably greater, partly because of unjust globalising structures, partly because of the AIDS epidemic.

Populorum Progressio seeks to foster the progressive development of all peoples. Its concern is that the structures of society be such that every person should be able to do more, learn more, and have more so that they might increase their personal worth (n. 6). HIV and AIDS go against all of this. Because of the way they permeate almost every facet of life in severely affected countries, they work powerfully against the common right of people to personal dignity and integral human development. Where prevalence rates are high, the epidemic traps individuals in a cycle where they can do less, learn less, have less, and become less – the very antithesis of the encyclical's vision of development.

What HIV and AIDS Do

Apart from the tragedy that they wreak on the life of an individual, HIV and AIDS do three things within society. They highlight existing problems, they magnify the scale and complexity of ongoing problems and they create new problems.

Like a very powerful spotlight, the epidemic draws attention to weaknesses, cracks and fault lines in many of society's structures and operations. One thinks of the lack of social protection mechanisms in communities at risk, the low health and nutritional status of poor people that increases their biological vulnerability to HIV infection, and the failure of law enforcement systems to protect women and children against sexual violence and possible subsequent HIV infection. The epidemic has also brought to the fore the widespread reality of sexual expression (Smith and McDonagh, 2003, p. 25); the way societies confront and often suppress issues of sexual orientation, and the ambivalence of society in dealing with deep-seated taboos surrounding blood, sex, and death and in confronting drug-injecting use.

But the epidemic is not content merely with drawing attention to these and other issues. It also increases their scale and makes them so complex that they almost defy solution. Thus, while every society is called on to respond to the needs of orphaned children, the AIDS epidemic has transformed this into an almost intractable problem in many countries where burgeoning numbers of orphans are placing family and community coping mechanisms under intense strain.

There is also a wide array of new problems, such as ensuring an unfailing supply of life-preserving but costly antiretroviral drugs for the millions who are in need; enabling elderly grandparents to assume a parenting role for grandchildren who are bereaved, impoverished, confused and extremely vulnerable; and overcoming the stigma and discrimination that have the triple effect of reducing the effectiveness of efforts to control the epidemic, creating an ideal climate for its further expansion, and undermining the very humanity of infected individuals to such an extent that some are driven to suicide.

Authentic Human Development

Real development is about improving the human situation. It seeks to create conditions in which people can lead productive, creative lives in keeping with their values, needs and interests. It is about ensuring that they can meet their basic needs for food, clean water, access to health and education services, and a decent standard of living. Making these situations a reality requires the expansion of physical infrastructure, the establishment of social and economic structures, and the development of functioning systems. But important as these may be, in the final analysis they are secondary. The primary meaning of development is increasing the capabilities and opportunities for individuals to take control of their own lives, meet their own needs, and live in dignity. In the words of *Populorum Progressio*, it is about enabling individuals to do more, learn more, and have more so that they might increase their personal worth (n. 6).

HIV and AIDS undercut this whole process. The most basic requirements for human development are that people should be able to lead long and healthy lives, be knowledgeable, have access to the resources needed to maintain a decent standard of living, and participate in the life of the community. In severely affected areas, AIDS can block the attainment of each one of these elements.

A Long and Healthy Life

Where HIV and AIDS are prevalent, they reduce people's prospects for a long and healthy life. Instead of rising, as it does in areas that are not so severely stricken, life expectancy declines steadily. In Zambia, for instance, the epidemic is believed to have reduced life expectancy at birth by about four years since 2000, and through the disease's continued impacts this will increase to eight years by 2010. Part of the reason is AIDS mortality which, in Zambia, is responsible for about 230 deaths each day.

But there are other effects that are hostile to life, with AIDS exploding the scale of other threats to health and well-being, such as tuberculosis, malaria and malnutrition. These impacts extend into the general population, beyond individuals infected with HIV. Areas where there is much AIDS are also areas where there is much tuberculosis. Malaria is intimately connected with HIV

THE CHALLENGE OF AIDS

infectivity and susceptibility, though AIDS prevention measures do not always take full account of this. HIV and AIDS frequently increase malnutrition, with adverse implications for people's vulnerability to other illnesses and for the growth and development of children. This is because the disease jeopardises household food security by reducing the income-earning and food-producing labour force, not only through sickness and deaths, but also through the time that productive adults must invest in caring for the sick.

At the same time, the epidemic has massive effects on already fragile health systems. It diverts limited health care facilities and personnel to the care and treatment of those who are HIV infected, thereby reducing capacity to respond to the whole range of other illnesses. It also causes severe reductions in the actual number of health care personnel who serve the poor in the public sector. These are lost to the public health system through AIDS-related sicknesses and deaths and through the movement of doctors, nurses, pharmacists and medical technicians out of the public sector to externally funded AIDS-related programmes.

Basic Education

Development is also about improving people's educational opportunities. It is about helping children go to school, stay in school, and learn through their school experiences. *Populorum Progressio* highlights 'learning more' as an aspect of development (n. 6). It further affirms that basic education is the first objective for any nation seeking to develop itself and that lack of education is as serious as lack of food (n. 35).

But HIV/AIDS puts this educational aspect of development under threat through its negative impacts on educators, learners and the overall learning environment. Like their medical counterparts, educators are succumbing to AIDS-related sicknesses and deaths. The result is classrooms without teachers and school systems without administrators.

The epidemic also influences the school participation of affected children. Some enrol late. Others attend only sporadically. Many do no not complete the full primary school cycle. Those who complete may not learn much, partly because of AIDS-related teacher non-availability, partly because of the emotional and psychological trauma that the disease has introduced into their lives, partly because they are so undernourished and in such poor general health that they are not able to learn. Unfortunately, the children who are in greatest need of all that schooling can offer, are the ones who are least likely to benefit – orphans, girls, those living with a disability, the poor, and children living with HIV.

The negative impacts of the epidemic on educational opportunities for young people are of special concern because of mounting evidence that greater exposure to school education results in significantly lower HIV rates. Young illiterate girls are among those who are most vulnerable to HIV infection. Denying them the opportunity of a complete school education not only denies their right to personal development: it also increases the possibility that they will become HIV infected.

The interaction between AIDS and education is two-way: AIDS makes the provision of education more difficult, but education makes the spread of HIV infection less likely. The way the epidemic affects the human body is strikingly similar to the way it affects an education system. In the body, HIV infection weakens and ultimately destroys the systems that have evolved so that the body can defend itself from within. In education, HIV likewise weakens and could ultimately destroy a system that is so protective that it has been designated as the social vaccine against HIV.

Development Conundrums Posed by HIV/AIDS
Education is not alone in the way it can be undermined by HIV/AIDS. The epidemic increases poverty, cripples health systems, and aggravates inequality. In doing so, it creates conditions favourable to increased transmission, reduced prevention, and less effective care, support and treatment. In biological terms, the virus can ensure its survival in the human body by developing resistance to the antiretroviral drugs used to prevent its replication. In social terms, the epidemic works towards its continuation by undermining the systems and institutions that offer protection.

This is one aspect of the difficult development conundrums with which HIV/AIDS confronts us. A further aspect is even more problematic. Development cannot occur without human capacity. Throughout the entire public, private, community and household sectors, however, AIDS is ravaging the capacities that are needed to bring about integral human development:

- Through sickness and death, the disease robs households, enterprises, services and sectors of qualified and experienced individuals.
- It creates the need for additional personnel (for example, in nursing or home-based care).
- It creates the need for persons with new understandings and skills (for example, personnel officers who must learn how to treat HIV and AIDS as important workplace issues).
- Because of the way it removes young and productive adults and parents, it reduces the capacity for the transfer of skills and for skills-formation in the next generation.

The challenge is how to achieve sustainable development under conditions where HIV and AIDS are destroying the capacities that are needed for such development. And in relation to the epidemic itself, the challenge is how to achieve the development needed for an effective response to the epidemic when HIV and AIDS are destroying the very capacities without which this response cannot occur.

HIV/AIDS and Poverty

Populorum Progression affirms that authentic development consists in the transition from less than human conditions to truly human ones (nn. 20–21). The less human conditions include the material poverty of those who lack the bare necessities of life and the moral poverty of those who are crushed by oppressive political and economic systems. Development occurs when such individuals experience movement from poverty to the acquisition of life's necessities. Thus, the third basic requirement for human development is that individuals have access to the resources needed to maintain a decent standard of living. But the close linkages between HIV/AIDS and poverty pose a constant threat to this movement from less to more human conditions.

AIDS is not a disease of poor countries. Neither is it a disease of poor people. However, where wealth is concentrated in the hands of a few, where the majority are so indigent that they cannot satisfy their basic needs, and where society is fragmented and not well organised, the scene is ripe for HIV and AIDS to make significant inroads. This is the situation in many parts of the world and within many of the severely affected countries. The experience of the past quarter century has shown the vulnerability of such an unequal global society to the onslaught of the epidemic.

As in other areas, there is a two-way interaction between HIV/AIDS and poverty: poverty worsens every aspect of the disease, while the disease worsens poverty. In a society with a generalised AIDS epidemic, poor people are, as a result of their circumstances, at higher risk of HIV infection than are the non-poor. This is because the poor may not be able to afford the time, medicines or treatment costs that would help to protect them against HIV infection. Because of their poverty, and as a survival strategy, poor women and children may have to trade sex for income, with all the attendant risks of becoming infected with HIV. Moreover, even in a highly subsidised social marketing situation, the poor are less likely to be able to afford condoms, and because of their living conditions they are also less likely to be able to store them properly, use them consistently, or apply them correctly.

In addition, the poor are more susceptible to HIV infection on health grounds. They are all too familiar with malnutrition, micronutrient deficiencies, malaria, tuberculosis, and infestation by bilharzia and other worms. Each one of these conditions depresses the immune system in such a way that in the event of a contact an individual becomes more easily HIV infected (and equally, an infected individual who experiences any one of these conditions is a more potent transmitter of HIV).

On social grounds, the poor, and especially poor women, frequently have a lower educational status, and thus have had limited access to what is acknowledged to be the only social vaccine against the disease. As a result, they tend to have less knowledge about the disease, how to protect themselves, the advantages of testing, and the medical services that are available.

Being poor also increases vulnerability. Poor people have few choices regarding their place and type of work, where they will live, their neighbours, what they will spend their money on, what they will eat, and how they will recreate themselves. Under pressure to meet immediate needs, they live for the present. They do not see that they have any future to protect and hence fail to appreciate the need to protect themselves against the possibility of HIV infection. To many, the prospect of AIDS sickness in eight or ten years' time is something so remote as to be unreal.

Because of HIV and AIDS the poor become poorer. This is due to the way the epidemic causes costs to rise, reduces incomes and resources, and necessitates the diversion of resources. Incomes and resources decline as jobs are lost through sickness or death; farm production is reduced; loans cannot be repaid; households headed by the elderly or children produce less; and the volume of sales declines because customers do not have resources to spare for anything but the most essential purchases. In addition, in order to survive many households may have to dispose of capital goods, among them productive assets such as animals, machinery or equipment, thereby imperilling their future productivity.

The cumulative effect of these various situations and lack of the necessary action is that poverty deepens and becomes more extensive. Instead of moving from less human to more human conditions, the state of the poor becomes even more wretched and their susceptibility to HIV infection becomes even more accentuated. Perhaps the oppressive face of HIV and AIDS is seen most clearly in the way it thrives off poverty and reinforces poverty. For AIDS-stricken countries and AIDS-stricken households, 'make poverty history' is more than a slogan. It is a cry from the hearts of oppressed people to be freed from the domination of the unjust and exploitative situations that bind them into poverty and tether them to HIV and AIDS.

Participation in the Life of the Community
Populorum Progressio reminds us that authentic human development cannot be restricted to economic growth alone (n. 14). Instead, it must foster the development of the whole person. A

person becomes a complete person only within the framework of society, a sentiment that re-echoes the saying of traditional African wisdom: a person is a person through other persons. Human self-fulfilment – being the architects of our own progress, taking control of our own lives, living with dignity, contributing to shaping our own future, and extending beyond ourselves in our legacy to future generations – sums up our aspirations. The realisation of these aspirations necessitates being able to attain self-fulfilment and enhance our sense of personal worth through full participation in the life of the community.

But here again, the sword of HIV / AIDS intervenes, cutting individuals off from the life of the community. It does so through the sicknesses that may make it impossible for an individual to achieve personal self-fulfilment as an active, productive member of a household and community. The malaise and sense of inadequacy that chronic illness may cause are compounded in the case of young productive adults as they grapple with unspoken questions, feelings of shame, self-doubt, guilt, self-blame, and extensive self-stigma. The feelings of lowered self-esteem, inferiority and utter helplessness that they experience give rise to deep inner suffering and a sense of isolation from the community and even at times from other family members.

But it is through the isolation and ostracism brought by externally enacted HIV / AIDS-related stigma and discrimination that infected individuals and their families come to feel that they do not belong. In a variety of ways and in every sort of gathering they can be made to feel discredited, reduced in value, branded as of lesser worth.

Why HIV / AIDS should give rise to such stigma is not altogether clear. Much has to do with the unspoken assumption of an association between HIV infection and morally disapproved behaviour, especially when this is sexual. Much comes from fear and ignorance, with people wanting to keep at a physical and social distance those infected with a disease that seems to be easily contracted (in fact, HIV does not transmit easily) and is a forerunner of major sickness and death (in fact, with today's improved knowledge and technologies both of these can be held at bay). Much is also coming from deep-seated concerns about having to deal with major human taboos. At the core of our being, we find it hard to accept that what should be the channels of new and ongoing life – sexual activity, seminal fluids, and blood – could also be channels of dehumanising sickness and death.

Because a person is a person through other persons, those who are stigmatised are denied the support and context they need for arriving at human self-fulfilment. By attacking the bonds that link people to one another, stigma and discrimination undercut the very humanity of infected individuals. This makes it difficult for them to maintain the self-esteem they need for full human living, to recognise that they are architects of their lives and destinies, to prove their self-worth through their accomplishments and by being themselves with their inherent and inalienable dignity.

As this wave of HIV/AIDS-related stigma and discrimination engulfs individuals and their families, it entrenches the disease. The epidemic goes underground, becoming hidden in an atmosphere of silence and denial, fertile ground for its further proliferation and hostile territory for its prevention and treatment.

National and Development Implications
Major implications of the AIDS epidemic in severely affected countries are, first, that national wealth grows at a slower rate than it would in the absence of the disease, and second, that a disproportionate amount of financial, human and social capital must be diverted to the HIV and AIDS response. Both factors constrain national development efforts. The epidemic has two other negative outcomes for development undertakings. It increases the costs of developments (because of the resources that must be ploughed into AIDS-related educational and care programmes) and it reduces the market for products (because responding to the disease uses many of the resources of affected would-be purchasers).

A further implication is the way HIV and AIDS affect the ability of the state to deliver services. In the private sector, low productivity on the part of an employee represents a cost to the organisation. In the public sector, however, low productivity is a cost to the people requiring the service. Though most prominent in the health, education and social welfare sectors, this reduced ability to deliver services can affect operations in every area and at every level of a state apparatus, and thereby reduce the ability to deliver on development obligations.

Finally, it is necessary to note that development activities themselves may facilitate the spread of HIV. *Populorum Progressio* warned that every kind of progress is a two-edged sword, necessary for fully human growth, but with potential to enslave (n. 19). This is very evident in the realm of HIV and AIDS. Increased and improved transport routes, enlarged markets, commercial farm developments, new mining ventures, major construction projects, and similar visible signs of development often involve large numbers of men living in close proximity to one another and away from their families. They also make possible the extensive movement of people. Both are sure markers for increased HIV vulnerability. The result is that areas of intense development activity may also be areas characterised by high HIV prevalence. The dilemma remains: how to promote development without at the same time promoting the spread of HIV and AIDS.

An Opportunity in Crisis
Clearly, HIV and AIDS pose a major challenge for development. Interactions between the two areas are intricate and involved, and indeed many of them have not yet been satisfactorily teased out. But even though many of the effects are calamitous, HIV and AIDS do not necessarily lead into a developmental cul-de-sac. On the contrary, the epidemic presents a special opportunity for growth, reform and improvement.

This is already happening in various spheres. In many rural and urban settings, vigorous community responses to the epidemic are revitalising society. In education, AIDS has created a greater sense of urgency in efforts to attain the Education-For-All goals. It is also stimulating a more comprehensive approach to the attainment of the Millennium Development Goals: there is increased recognition that progress towards each goal must also involve progress towards slowing down the spread of HIV and that failure to attain the goal of slowing the spread of HIV jeopardises the attainment of all of the others.

Because of its extensive and disproportionate impact on women and girls, the epidemic has signalled greater global concern about the scandal of gender inequity and has triggered more extensive and coordinated efforts to find ways for putting an end to every form of gender discrimination. It is also leading to a greater awareness of the extent of violence, child abuse, and different forms of sexual orientation.

Critically, in the field of development itself, the epidemic has focused attention on the need for a more extended approach that goes beyond the surface drivers of HIV transmission (sexual behaviour, infected blood products, mother-to-child transmission, and injecting-drug use) and pays attention instead to the development, health, education and welfare environment within which these drivers operate. 'The HIV epidemic is not an isolated event. It is the predictable result of declining economies, insecure food systems, and inadequate investment in water, sanitation, health care, and education' (Stillwaggon, 2006, p. 167).

The relentless expansion of the epidemic presents an opportunity to adopt this developmental focus. It challenges us to extend our vision beyond narrow attention to the virus to understanding HIV and AIDS as a developmental issue. It calls on every actor to use international, national and local resources to enhance the holistic development of individuals and communities, and thereby create an environment within which the proliferation of HIV and AIDS becomes less likely.

In other words, the epidemic calls for the 'progressive development of peoples who are trying to escape the ravages of hunger, poverty, endemic disease and ignorance; of those who are seeking a larger share in the benefits of progress and a more active improvement of their human qualities; of those who are consciously striving for fuller growth' (n. 1).

HIV / AIDS is more than a health or a behavioural problem. It is a development problem. It is essential that it be responded to as such. AIDS can be overcome, but only if development and the epidemic mutually com-penetrate each other in seeking to promote the movement of peoples from less to more human conditions.

References

Smith, Ann and Enda McDonagh (2003), *The Reality of HIV/AIDS*, Maynooth: Trócaire.

Stillwaggon, Eileen (2006), 'The Ecology of Poverty: Nutrition, Parasites, and Vulnerability to HIV/AIDS', in Stuart Gillespie (ed) *AIDS, Poverty and Hunger: Challenges and Responses*, Washington DC: International Food Policy Research Institute, 167–179.

Will the Twain Ever Meet?
Gender and Development

Maria Riley OP

Reading *Populorum Progressio* 40 years later leads one to ponder what the world would be like today if Pope Paul VI's vision of authentic human development and global solidarity had been implemented. In some ways, the encyclical is the triumph of hope and idealism over realism and worldly wisdom, a criticism the Pope anticipated (n. 79). Unfortunately, *Populorum Progressio* has proved more prophetic in its predictions of the problems ahead, than successful in winning acceptance for its reflections and prescriptions to individuals, institutions and governments on directions to move if authentic development is to be realised.

The encyclical is truly prescient in predicting future problems. Before developing world debt ballooned in the 1970s into the debt crisis which still remains today, Pope Paul was warning of the need to manage financial assistance before countries become 'overwhelmed by debt whose repayment swallows up the greater part of their gains' (n. 54). Likewise, he identified the failures of the current model of trade liberalisation and pointed out that contracts between unequal parties can be unfair even if entered into with mutual consent (n. 59). His 1967 critique of 'free trade' could have been written today. Some 20 years before the demise of communism and the global turn to neoliberal economic solutions, Pope Paul identified 'unbridled liberalism' as leading to a particular type of tyranny, the 'international imperialism of money' (n. 26). He also identified issues with which countries are grappling today: racism, the sovereign right of nations to chart their own path of development, social unrest, massive outward migration, ethnic tensions and wars fuelled by people's poverty and lack of opportunity. He worried about the sickness of society – greed, the abuse of power, materialism – that stifle the soul just as extreme poverty and lack of opportunity stifle the spirit. We are living in such times now with no road map through them because the world community ignored the maps suggested by *Populorum Progressio*. It is time to return to those maps and reintroduce them in the early 21st century setting.

Two current issues not foreseen by Pope Paul VI would need to be introduced. They are environmental limits and gender justice. My task in this chapter is to address gender justice. But first an historical aside: Pope Paul VI was not alone in his failure to see the issue of gender in development. *Populorum Progressio* was written in 1967. The first major work on the issues of women in development was Ester Boserup's groundbreaking book, *Woman's Role in Economic Development*, published in 1970. This book began the amazing work of bringing women into visibility as key actors not only in the household but also in the productive economy. In this chapter, I will trace the evolution of women in development both in theory and in action, reflect on how the reality of women's role in development would have added to *Populorum Progressio* and identify how subsequent encyclicals have dealt with the issue.

Let us look at Pope Paul VI's approach to gender as reflected in some of his other writings. Paul VI was in line with the historic view of women and men that frames Vatican documents. Simply put, it is an essentialist view of women and men. Its anthropology reflects a 'biology is destiny' perspective. Because women are capable of bearing children, that is assumed to be their primary role in the human community. Men's primary role is to support the family and hence to be the head of the family, reflecting the Fatherhood of God. Man and woman's biological complementarity defines the male/female relationship in all other spheres. In Vatican documents, women's world, capabilities and opportunities are circumscribed by phrases such as 'according to her appropriate role or according to her nature'. Men are never described with like limitations on their nature and roles. This approach raises the question as to whether the church implicitly subscribes to a dual human nature: man's nature, which is normative and open and woman's nature, which is determined by her ability to bear children. This particular view has been strongly criticised by feminist theologians, ethicists and scholars (Cahill, 2005; Johnson, 2004; Riley, 1994 and 2005).

However, Pope Paul VI and his predecessors were not alone in their view. The 'development experts' who directed the UN Development Decades (1960s and 1970s) were primarily white, educated, males of European descent from the middle classes of their societies. They took the mid-twentieth century western middle class woman as the model for all women of the world, a model that did not fit the reality of women in the developing world. Hence their approach to women in development was a social welfare model. Women were seen as passive beneficiaries of development. The goal was to bring women into development as better mothers in order to fulfil better their primary role (Moser, 1993). The field was ripe for some focused research on the reality of the lives and roles of women in developing countries.

Women in the Development Process

In *Woman's Role in Economic Development*, Ester Boserup introduced to a wide audience the reality of women's lives in the developing world by examining four main areas of that world: Africa, Arab countries, South and East Asia, and Latin America. She argued that women were not only being marginalised from their traditional roles and activities by the process of development, but that women were not taken into account for their contributions to development. Nor, contrary to conventional wisdom, were women enjoying the presumed gains from development (Antrobus, 2004). The study met a small but dedicated and ready audience. The so-called third wave of the women's movement had been growing in the US and across Europe during the 1960s and there was a cadre of women in UN and national development and aid agencies that had begun to look at what was happening to women across the globe. Boserup's book provided the impetus and the initial information needed to focus the issues.

In the ensuing years, the understanding of women in development has evolved as women sought to define their own lives and roles and organised to promote the advancement of women in both the developing and the so-called developed worlds. The multiple tasks were not easy, either conceptually or politically. Nor are they yet finished.

The United Nations was the key institution in promoting the advancement of women globally through its sponsorship of the Decade for Women (1975-1985) and the four World Conferences for Women related to the decade: Mexico City (1975), Copenhagen (1980), Nairobi (1985) and Beijing (1995). The Conferences afforded women from all parts of the world the political space to learn from each other, debate issues and approaches, influence each other's positions, form alliances, influence government and institutional policies and emerge as a powerful global movement to challenge existing political, economic, social and cultural issues. The history of these Conferences is a fascinating story of building a social movement and a political agenda, but it is beyond the scope of this chapter.

Women in development (WID) was one of the central concepts shaping debates throughout this period of time as women sought an adequate analytical framework to conceptualise the problems and to develop a political agenda for change. The meaning of 'women in development' was the first issue. The aphorism 'Where you stand depends a great deal on where you sit' is apt for understanding this debate.

The WID approach was developed primarily by women working in a variety of development institutions, primarily in the North, such as the UN, the World Bank, national Aid offices and Women's Bureaux. It was supported by academic researchers, development professionals and practitioners. The WID approach targets women with specific policies and programmes to address their particular needs such as education, maternal health care, or access to training and resources in order 'to integrate them into the development process'. It focuses its work on the micro level of development. It assumes that the reigning development paradigm is basically good and leading to economic growth. Its primary concern is to integrate women into that process and ensure they reap the benefits (Randriamaro, 2006). The WID approach was the official reigning approach during the 1970s and 1980s. It was accepted without question by the majority of women in development NGOs in the North.

144

However, from the beginning, women from the developing world challenged the WID approach. First of all, they argued that women were already 'integrated' into the development process and that it was subjecting them to subordination and exploitation. They questioned what kind of development was needed to address women's concerns. They faulted their Northern colleagues for assuming that the capitalist model of development was benign. They were frustrated that the Northern women had command of the research field on women in the developing world. In 1976, African women took the first steps in producing their own work with the forming of the African Association for Women and Development (AAWORD). Other women in the developing world followed, establishing their own research programmes and producing alternative analyses of development and the reality of women in the development process (Antrobus, 2004).

Another controversial issue was the meaning and use of feminist analysis as a framing ideology. Many women in the developing world rejected feminism as a Northern imposition on the global women's agenda. This position was reinforced by their governments and male colleagues. The objections often related to an inadequate understanding of feminism and the reality that liberal feminism was the reigning ideology in the North. Liberal feminism, with its emphasis on women's equality and uncritical acceptance of capitalism, also supported the WID approach. In 1985, at the Third World Conference on Women, DAWN, an organisation of prominent scholars and activists from the developing world, defined a feminism which reflected a different approach in their book *Development, Crises, and Alternative Visions: Third World Women's Perspectives* (Sen and Grown, 1985). The book was a compelling indictment of the neoliberal process of development as fostered by the international financial institutions and the powerful industrial economies. Its authors proposed a vision of feminism that has 'at its very core a process of economic and social development geared to human needs through wider control over and access to economic and political power'. They insisted that while gender subordination has universal elements, there must be a 'diversity of feminisms, responsive to the different needs and concerns of different women, and *defined by them for themselves'* (Sen and Grown, 1985, italics in original). This definition bridged the differences between Northern and Southern feminists and opened the way for women to challenge all forms of marginalisation, including sexism, racism, homophobia, economic class and neocolonialism. It continues to be the working definition for feminist economists and activists today.

From WID to GAD (Gender and Development)

The failure of the WID approach in addressing the inequalities between women and men led to a greater emphasis on gender differences, paving the way for a new approach called gender and development (GAD). GAD uses gender, rather than women, as an analytical category to understand how economic, political, social and cultural systems affect women and men differently. Gender is defined as the social roles, expectations and responsibilities assigned to women and men because of their biological differences. It is an ideological and cultural construct that can change over time and across cultures.

The GAD approach signals three important departures from WID. First, it identifies the unequal power relations between women and men. Second, it re-examines all social, political and economic structures and development policies from the perspective of gender differences. And third, it recognises that achieving gender equality and equity will demand transformative change (United Nations, 1999). The GAD approach demands transformative change in gender relations from the household to global politics and policy and within all mediating institutions, such as the World Bank, the IMF, WTO and national governments.

At the household level, the gendered division of labour traditionally defines women's role primarily as family maintenance – social reproduction. This work is unpaid, taken for granted and invisible in economic terms, but has significant impact on the quality of women's lives as well as on social well-being and economic progress. When women enter the paid workforce, they assume the 'double work day', paid and unpaid. The invisibility of women's unpaid work remains a critical issue in national and international policy. For example, the application of IMF and World Bank stabilisation and structural adjustment policies (SAPs) caused many countries to cut back on government-sponsored or subsidised social services. Women bear the burden when public sector services switch to the household, increasing the amount of unpaid work on their already stretched energy and resources.

However, although GAD represents an increasingly more accurate and critical analysis of the impact of neoliberal development on women, it does not necessarily address the neoliberal development paradigm that is being fostered by the World Bank, the IMF and the WTO. Because it remains focused on the imbalances in gender relations and so called gender-blind policies, it tends to overlook the 'systemic imbalances between developing and developed countries, as well as the structural problems in the global governance of macroeconomic policies generally ...' (Randriamaro, 2006).

Beyond GAD, women have been demanding the full exercise of their human rights and are developing a rights-based approach to economic policy. In the June 2000 issue of *World Development*, Caren Grown, Diane Elson and Nilufer Cagatay advocate 'a rights-based approach to economic policy which aims directly at strengthening the realisation of human rights, which include social, economic and cultural rights, as well as civil and political rights. Such an approach goes beyond viewing gender concerns as instrumental to growth, as is sometimes the case, because it recognises women's agency and their rights and obligations as citizens' (Grown, Elson and Cagatay, 2000). This approach clearly illustrates a profound political shift in the Global Women's Movement that became evident at the Fourth World Conference on Women (1995), where women were no longer focusing on a narrow range of so-called women's issues, but were demanding a voice in all arenas of economic policy-making.

A Feminist Political Economy Alternative
The insights from the various frameworks analysing women's role in economic life – WID, GAD and human rights – are currently evolving and coalescing into a feminist political economy

as the most comprehensive frame for debate and advocacy for economic justice and security for women as well as for men, families and communities, in the globalising economy. A feminist political economic analysis places the questions of power and gender expectations at the centre.

The issue of power addresses the power imbalances in all dimensions and spheres of human activity. These dynamics include the gender power equation at the household level, as well as the power equations at the meso levels that are not only gendered, but also reflect racial, ethnic and economic class power imbalances. In macroeconomics, it addresses the power imbalance in current neoliberal and neocolonial economic dynamics fostered by the international financial institutions and trade and investment liberalisation.

The analysis of gender expectations examines the imbalance in social roles and expectations between women and men in various societies and cultural settings. It also reveals patterns of discrimination against women in all societies that continue to relegate them to secondary positions in all dimensions of human activity. 'A (feminist) political economy approach emphasises the crucial need to link trade policy, fiscal, monetary, industrial and social policies alongside an analysis of global inequities' if gender equity and sustainable human development are to be realised (Randriamaro, 2006).

Populorum Progressio and Feminist Political Economy

Given the historical disjuncture between the writing of *Populorum Progressio* and the field of women in economic development, a question presents itself: how might the encyclical be different if Pope Paul VI had been exposed to the questions and frameworks that women bring to the development debate? Two issues come immediately to mind: the issue of power, and of including women as subjects, not only of development but of authentic human life.

Populorum Progressio does raise the issue of power in several places; for example, it speaks of 'flagrant inequalities ... even more in the exercise of power' (n. 9) and 'oppressive political structures resulting ... [in] the improper exercise of power' (n.

21). But there is no analysis of power as a structural cause of underdevelopment. It was the Latin American bishops, taking their lead from Paul VI, who recognised and articulated how politics shaped development. This recognition led them to advocate liberation rather then development, realising that the main obstacles to human development were oppressive and non-participatory governments (Figueroa, 2005).

From the beginning of their struggle to achieve full personhood and equal opportunity in the society as well as in the church, women were confronted with the issue of power. Patriarchy, the system of rule by men, is historically entrenched in all social structures and the majority of cultural and religious systems around the world. In their liberation struggle, women have had to analyse the structures of power in order to determine how to address them effectively. It has been a challenging and often painful task and the work is far from over. The axiom that the powerful do not give over their power, it must be taken from them, has proved true more often than not. Although Pope Paul recognised the imbalance of power, *Populorum Progressio* only used reasoned arguments and moral imperatives to address that imbalance. As history has shown, that approach has proved inadequate and the encyclical today is a document of vision and unfulfilled hope.

Equally important is the understanding that women are subjects of economic development and authentic human life. Reading the encyclical is a very painful exercise for anyone whose consciousness regarding the equality and mutuality of women and men has been changed over the past 40 years. The repeated use of 'man's' authentic development, while it can be dismissed as an historical use of generic language, is also a reminder that too much ecclesiastical and secular writing and speaking today still does not fully incorporate women as meaningful participants in all dimensions of life. Using generic language continues to render too many women invisible and denies their full personhood. Had Pope Paul included women as well as men in his descriptions of authentic human development, how much richer his reflections would have been.

He would also have found strong allies among women to buttress his arguments that social development is as important as economic development and that it often precedes economic development by producing an educated, healthy citizenry who bring energy and creativity to the world. While that fact is recognised today, especially among women, the reality continues that social development is the first target of budget cutbacks.

However, what is more disconcerting than *Populorum Progressio*'s virtual silence on women is the lack of gender awareness and inclusivity in subsequent encyclicals. The evolution of the role of women in economic development from WID to the current feminist political economy has had very little impact on the development of social encyclicals over the past 40 years. Pope John Paul II and Pope Benedict XVI (then Cardinal Ratzinger) have both written statements about women but they have been on the margins of the main body of Catholic social teaching. For example, they never show up in any compendium of that teaching. Two examples are *Mulieris Dignitatem* (John Paul II, 1988) and the *Letter to the Bishops of the Catholic Church on the Collaboration of Men and Women in the Church and in the World* (Congregation for the Doctrine of the Faith, 2004). Each of these documents seeks to address the 'women's question' in the contemporary world. Cardinal Ratzinger's relies heavily on Pope John Paul II's document. They both maintain an essentialist understanding of woman, her primary role of motherhood and her feminine values while they struggle to recognise women's new and emerging role in societies across the globe.

However, the documents continue to make women's capacity for bearing children the defining factor of their lives. In naming 'feminine values' they universalise and idealise women. They invite women to bring their special values to humanise society, but what does this say implicitly about men? The problem with both documents is that they speak only to women's identity and roles in the family and society. They do not speak to men's identity and roles. They present an exalted sense of the 'genius of women', and in so doing diminish men. They base their arguments of complementarity on sexual difference and union, but fail to speak to the wholeness and integrity of each human person and the mutuality in relationships that wholeness should call forth.

Catholic social teaching has a wealth of insight on the fundamental issues of a just society, authentic human development, human rights and the dignity of the human person that would enrich feminist political economics. However, feminist women have important dimensions and insights to bring to Catholic social teaching regarding the structured nature of gender roles and social reproduction, as well as a critical analysis of economic liberalisation and development that would enrich that teaching. These insights could have a transformative effect on economic and social development. However, until the official church becomes more open to honest dialogue with women, those insights and strengths will remain outside the stream of Catholic social teaching and that body of teaching will be the weaker for it.

References

Antrobus, Peggy (2004) *The Global Women's Movement: Origins, Issues and Strategies*, Kingston, Jamaica: Ian Randle Publishers.

Boserup, Ester (1970) *Women's Role in Economic Development*, New York: St Martin's Press Inc.

Cahill, Lisa Sowle (2004) 'Familiaris Consortio', in Kenneth R. Himes, OFM (ed) *Modern Catholic Social Teaching: Commentaries and Interpretations*, Washington, DC: Georgetown University Press.

Congregation for the Doctrine of the Faith (2004) *Letter to the Bishops of the Catholic Church on the Collaboration of Men and Women in the Church and in the World*, 31 May 2004.

Deck, Allan Figueroa (2004) 'Populorum Progressio', in Kenneth R. Himes, OFM (ed) *Modern Catholic Social Teaching: Commentaries and Interpretations*, Washington, DC: Georgetown University Press.

Grown, Caren, Diane Elson and Nilufer Cagatay (2000) 'Introduction', *World Development*, 28:7, July 2000.

Johnson, Elizabeth (2004) *Truly Our Sister: A Theology of Mary in the Communion of Saints,* New York: Continuum International Publishing Group Inc.

Moser, Caroline O.N. (1993) *Gender Planning and Development: Theory, Practice and Training*, London: Routledge.

Pope John Paul II (1988) *Mulieris Dignitatem* (The Dignity and Vocation of Women), Apostolic Letter, 15 August 1988.

Randriamaro, Zo (2006) 'Gender and Trade: Overview Report' (online). Available at: URL: http://www.bridge.ids.ac.uk/reports/CEP-TRADE-OR.pdf. (Accessed 10 May 2006)

Riley, Maria (1994) 'Women', in J. Dwyer (ed) *The New Dictionary of Catholic Social Thought*, Collegeville, MN: The Liturgical Press.

Riley, Maria (2005) 'Engendering the Pastoral Circle', in Frans Wijsen, Peter Henriot and Rodrigo Mejia (eds) *The Pastoral Circle Revisited: A Critical Quest for Truth and Transformation*, Maryknoll, NY: Orbis Books.

Sen, Gita and Caren Grown (1985) *Development, Crises and Alternative Visions: Third World Women's Perspectives*, Stavanger, Norway: A. S. Verbum.

United Nations (1999) *1999 World Survey on the Role of Women in Development: Globalization, Gender and Work*, Report to the Secretary General, New York: United Nations Publications.

Human Rights:
A Contemporary Development Challenge

Mulima Kufekisa-Akapelwa

Introduction

When asked to contribute to this book that is intended to commemorate the 40th anniversary of Pope Paul VI's encyclical *Populorum Progressio*, I was rather uncertain and hesitant. I am neither a theologian nor an expert in Catholic social teaching (CST). However, since I have been associated with the power of CST for the past 10 years in my work at the Catholic Centre for Justice, Development and Peace (CCJDP) in Zambia, I decided to give it a try.

I was asked to write on 'Human Rights: A Contemporary Development Challenge'. Being situated in a developing country context, such a topic readily yields many examples. The real challenge, however, would be to present the Zambian context of the prevalent denial and lack of fulfilment of rights of the people of God in such a way as to still show hope for the future.

The first part of my chapter looks at what Human Rights (HR) are, specifically presenting the Universal Declaration of Human Rights (UDHR) and the Economic, Social and Cultural Rights (ESCR), and shows how they have now become a normative framework. A look is also taken at the way HR have been promoted in the past and how a dichotomy emerged between the promotion of civil and political rights on the one hand and economic, social and cultural rights on the other hand.

The relationship between human rights and development is discussed in the second part, where it is clearly seen that the respect and upholding of human rights is an imperative for any genuine development.

The last part of the article discusses the challenges in meeting key human rights that would unlock the potential of persons and therefore enable them to attain expanded freedoms and to that end, development. In selecting key human rights one does not argue that these are the only important ones. For indeed human rights discourse always emphasises the indivisibility and inalienability of rights.

What are Human Rights?

It is commonly affirmed that human rights are universal, equal and inalienable. All human beings hold them universally, simply on the grounds that they are human. One either is or is not human and thus has or does not have human rights. And one can no more lose these rights than one can stop being human – no matter how inhuman the treatment one may suffer. One is entitled to human rights and one is empowered by them. This shows clearly that human rights arise out of one's humanity. *Populorum Progressio* reflects this understanding from the start of the document where the position on the imperative of the development of peoples is made: 'If the world is made to furnish each individual with the means of livelihood and the instruments for their growth and progress, each person has therefore the right to find in the world what is necessary for themselves' (n. 22). From this it is clear that human rights are not earned or given or granted. Rather they are inherent in an individual by virtue of one's humanity.

Society has over time agreed on these rights and they are now codified in a Universal Declaration of 1948. This was the first agreement globally achieved under the auspices of the United Nations. Following that 1948 Declaration, covenants respecting various rights and freedoms were signed by governments. These related to discrimination (1965), torture (1984), women (1976) children (1989), civil and political rights (1966), and economic, social and cultural rights (1966).

Over time there has been a discrepancy in the way these rights have been promoted and upheld. This was not the intention of the people who gathered at the UN to first proclaim the Universal Declaration of Human Rights. However, with the onset of the Cold War, rights were promoted differently in the West and in the East. The former emphasised civil and political rights and the latter emphasised economic and social rights – with cultural rights being neglected.

For the developing countries that related to both Eastern and Western blocs, these biases were inherent in the development cooperation received. International and local human rights groups in developing countries tended to work exclusively on issues of torture, freedom of speech, freedom of association, women's rights, civil and political rights. Not much work was done on economic, social and cultural rights. It was not until the 1990s that there began to be shifts in the emphasis to more practically cover the economic, social and cultural rights. The UN body itself adopted a new agreement 'The Right to Development'. This brought together the contents of the Covenant of Civil and Political Rights and the Covenant of Economic, Social and Cultural Rights.

Overleaf is a summary of the content of the Covenants, showing the specific right to which the individual is entitled. It should be borne in mind that the Covenants also indicate what State parties and society are obliged to do. The list is not exhaustive of the respective Covenants. There are other rights elucidated in other conventions, including civil and political rights, women's rights, the rights of the child, the right to be free from torture, discrimination and so on. For the purposes of this chapter I will dwell on economic, social and cultural rights.

Forty years ago, Paul VI summed up these rights and pointed to these issues in *Populorum Progressio*, recognising that:

> Freedom from misery, the greater assurance of finding subsistence, health and fixed employment; an increased share of responsibility without oppression of any kind and in security from situations that do violence to their dignity as human beings; better education – in brief, to seek to do more, know more and have more in order to be more; this is what men and women aspire to now… (n. 6)

Human Rights and Development

To understand human rights as a development challenge, it is necessary to look at what development is and how or whether it is a component of current human rights provisions. In discussing development I will focus on development as it relates to the improvement of the life of the human person. In this way, of course, I am simply reiterating the Catholic social teaching's emphasis on the human person. All development has to be for the

UNIVERSAL DECLARATION OF HUMAN RIGHTS (UDHR)	ECONOMIC, SOCIAL AND CULTURAL RIGHTS (ESCRS)
Each person is born free and equal	Equality of men and women to enjoyment of all economic, social and cultural rights
Right to life, liberty and security of person	
None shall be held in servitude and slavery	Rights to work, right of everyone to the opportunity to gain living by work freely chosen
Freedom from torture, cruelty and inhuman treatment	Right to enjoyment of just and favourable conditions of work
Equality before the law	Right to form trade unions
Freedom of movement	Right to strike
Freedom to hold nationality	Right to social security
Right to found a family	Protection and assistance to the family
Free full consent to marriage	Freedom to enter into marriage
Right to own property	Protection of children and young adults from economic and social exploitation
Right to freedom of thought and religion	
Right to peaceful assembly	Right to an adequate standard of living, including adequate food, clothing and housing and to continuous improvement of living conditions
Not compelled to belong to an association	
Equal access to public services	
Right to social security	Freedom from hunger
Right to work, free choice of employment, just and favourable conditions of work and protection against unemployment	Right to highest attainable standard of physical and mental health
	Right to education
Right to equal pay for equal work	Right to take part in cultural life
Just and favourable remuneration ensuring the worker and family an existence worthy of human dignity	Right to enjoy benefits of scientific progress and its applications
Right to join a union	
Right to leisure including reasonable working hours	
Rights to a standard of living adequate for health and well being of self and family, including food, clothing, housing and medical care and necessary social services	
Right to education	
Special care for motherhood and childhood	

benefit of the human person, at the service of that person, and not vice versa.

What is development then? Development is now taken to mean improving the lives and well-being of people so that they can attain their full potential. Earlier understandings of development primarily emphasised the economic aspect, an aspect mainly measured by a country's Gross National Product (GNP) or, at the individual level, by income. The United Nations Development Programme (UNDP) has, since the early 1990s, challenged this narrow economic emphasis. Their annual *Human Development Reports* focus more on the full range of human capabilities. Therefore a measure of development would include access to education, freedom from hunger, access to good health, opportunities for livelihood and employment, participation and voice in decision-making, and other indicators of well-being. It is highly significant to note, therefore, that Paul VI stated this emphasis on the full range of rights and capabilities when he gave very simple but highly profound definitions: '… authentic development, a development which is for each and all the transition from less human conditions to those which are more human' (n. 22) and 'Development cannot be limited to mere economic growth. In order to be authentic, it must be complete: integral, that is, it has to promote the good of every person and of the whole person' (n. 14).

What do Human Rights and Human Development have in Common?

The UNDP 2000 *Human Development Report*, which dealt with the topic 'Human Rights and Human Development', stated that:

> Human rights and human development share a common vision and a common purpose – to secure the freedom, well-being and dignity of all people everywhere. To secure:

- Freedom from discrimination, by gender, race, ethnicity, nationality, region or religion
- Freedom from want – to enjoy a decent standard of living
- Freedom to develop and realise one's human potential
- Freedom from fear – of threats to personal security, from torture, arbitrary arrests and other violent acts
- Freedom from injustice and violations of the rule of law

- Freedom of thought and speech and to participate in decision-making and to form associations
- Freedom for decent work without exploitation.
(UNDP, 2000)

This understanding of the close relationship between human rights and human development as freedoms is central to the thinking of Nobel Prize laureate Amartya Sen in his classic treatise, *Development as Freedom* (Sen, 1999). Sen gives the well-being of humans centre stage in the drama of development, emphasising what he calls 'capabilities'. Freedoms, he argues, are not only the primary end of development but they are also among its principal means. For Sen, development should be seen as a process of expanding freedoms. And freedoms are precisely what human rights aim for.

Freedom upholds the centrality of human dignity. This complete understanding of development, that it is freedom from several wants, is indeed akin to the ideas of Paul VI. In his emphasis that development has to be integral, the Pope quotes the great French Dominican, L.-J. Lebret: 'We do not believe in separating the economic from the human, nor development from the civilisations in which it exists. What we hold important is the human person, each person and each group of people, and we even include the whole of humanity' (n. 14).

What is the State of Human Development?

The full achievement of these freedoms, judging from the current state of world development almost 60 years since the Universal Declaration of Human Rights, is indeed a huge challenge. It is fundamentally a development challenge. It is a challenge that was fully recognised by Paul VI in *Populorum Progressio*:

> Today the principal fact that we must all recognise is that the social question has become worldwide. John XXIII stated this in unambiguous terms and the Council echoed him in its *Pastoral Constitution on the Church in the Modern World*. This teaching is important and its application urgent. Today the peoples in hunger are making a dramatic appeal to the peoples blessed with abundance. The church shudders at this cry of anguish and calls each one to give a loving response of charity to their brothers' and sisters' cries for help. (n. 3)

This challenge, stated 40 years ago, is certainly still with us, as evidenced by the poor situation of men, women, youth and children in so many parts of the world today. The world is plagued by insecurity, hunger and deprivation, with millions of children dying of malnutrition. Preventable disease still reigns in the developing world. The HIV/AIDS pandemic is overwhelming in poor countries. The majority of people in urban areas live in inhuman conditions lacking proper shelter, sanitation and water. Women in the developing world are denied opportunities for equal participation. Too many children are not in school, young adults are lacking the opportunities for training that might afford them a better life, unemployment is rife. The informal sector – where many people survive by selling goods on the street – is unable to absorb the surplus labour. The list of challenges is endless, quite desperate and discouraging.

What is needed to achieve these freedoms?
I write from the perspective of Zambia, a country of immense potential but a country that scores 166 out of 177 nations on the UNDP Human Development Index. Writing from that perspective, I would propose the following emphases that link human rights, freedoms and development:

- An ingrained respect for human rights in the wider sense in both government officials and the wider populace
- An increased awareness-building effort aimed at the poor and their allies to emphasise the rights and duties of individuals, state parties and others
- The generation of practical policies and programmes for reaching the poorest
- A priority on public expenditure that achieves real results
- An investment in education, not only primary but secondary and tertiary as well

1. An Ingrained Culture of Human Rights
An ingrained respect of human rights could be called a 'culture of human rights'. Written as it is, this might seem simplistic and simply a borrowing from the development trend with its cliché of a 'rights-based approach'. Simple as this statement might initially appear, it is loaded with potential. Governments and people in many developing countries do not have a culture of respect

for human rights. This is shown in the fact that many countries have not guaranteed economic, social and cultural rights in their constitutions. Indeed, Zambia is a case in point, attesting to this lack of an 'ingrained culture'.

People are dubious about the ability of a government to guarantee these rights, as the actual record of safeguarding rights seems dismal. In almost all Zambian elections since the re-introduction of multiparty politics (1991), the politicians always urge the electorate to vote for their party or otherwise: 'Development will not come to their areas!' This is not only a blatant disregard for the ideal of striving through all means possible to progressively bring improvements in the living standards of the people, it is also a direct denial of the basic human right of development – something that is not dependent on the goodwill of politicians.

Very high levels of poverty are prevalent in a majority of the developing countries (for example, in Zambia 67 per cent of people live below the poverty line). Yet there is not a popular culture of people fighting for their rights. People do not ask: 'Why is there no "development"?' They do not ask why there are poor expenditure patterns that deprive the people of their right to better living conditions. If such a culture of human rights was ingrained in the people, however, without even having legal recourse, there would be a stronger adherence to the principles of implementation by governments. This would work because there would be pressure from the bottom up on the government and other parties to uphold and respect economic and social rights.

Among the most deprived categories in Zambia are the urban poor, dwelling in what are officially categorised as slum areas. Over 60 per cent of the population in the capital Lusaka live in such areas – with minimal access to water, sanitation, health facilities and schools. The populace relies on unstable livelihoods such as stone crushing and gets by with very low literacy levels. All too often, however, this way of life is taken as the norm. The people living in these conditions do not readily see their situation as a violation of their basic human rights. Civil society organisations working to deal with these problems usually focus attention on improving such conditions by providing community-based schools and other similar amenities, but the use of the power of a people informed about their rights is missing.

Developing an ingrained culture of human rights among people may seem to be a long-term vision. To many people, it may seem as something very unrealistic. However, it must be worked at if we are to build societies that stand up for their rights so that the freedoms of development can be achieved. This is a real challenge especially in countries where education and literacy levels are still very low. Developing such a culture could be a long process but many civil society groups are now more involved in issues related to economic, social and cultural rights. With widespread availability of communication such as community radio stations, it is possible to build this culture.

2. Increased Awareness-building amongst the Poor about Rights and the Duties of the Individual and Others
This proposal looks at the medium to long-term range of responses, something that was explicitly recognised by Paul VI as stated in *Populorum Progressio* when he emphasised that as a

> contribution to this great cause of peoples in development, we considered it our duty to set up a Pontifical Commission in the Church's central administration, charged with 'bringing to the whole of God's People the full knowledge of the part expected of them at the present time, so as to further the progress of poorer peoples, to encourage social justice among nations, to offer to less developed nations the means whereby they can further their own progress': its name, which is also its programme, is Justice and Peace. (n. 5)

3. Practical Policies and Programmes for reaching the Poorest
This is very much a core message of Paul VI in calling for action, commitment and solidarity as they relate to social questions. All too often policies for the poor have been developed in such a way that it is not easy to effectively reach the poor. In addition, the challenges of working with the poor are usually left to a few Non-Governmental Organisations (NGOs) who have only limited access to the poor. Even when they record novel ways of reaching the poorest, these are often not then adopted by the public sector.

The capacity and size of the public sector in a developing country is another issue of concern. For over two decades now the state has been under attack from the Bretton Woods institutions (World Bank and International Monetary Fund) calling for a 're-treat of the state', meaning a small public sector base. Due to the impact of such policies over the years, the capacity of the public sector to reach the poorest has become very limited and often very ineffective.

Some other constraints in reaching the poor lie in the failure of a developing country's policies to enhance growth in its local private sector. Such a growth would enable more jobs to be generated in an economy. In Zambia, the situation is that tax policies favour foreign investors more highly than local businesses. Yet conditions offered by these foreign companies to workers often do not guarantee a just wage, provide safe working situations or enhance local living environments. Such conditions certainly do not respect rights or promote development. This indicates that there is need for local civil society to engage in such issues in order to widen the possible sources of livelihood and employment for the poor.

4. Public Expenditure that Achieves Real Results
The quality of public expenditure in a developing country is of great potential in meeting the freedoms of development. Such quality relates to the efficiency and effectiveness of spending. It is not only these variables that are important but also the accountability and transparent manner of public expenditure management. Why is this an important issue for the attainment of full human rights and development? And why is it a challenge?

It is obvious that most policy programmes need money in order to be achieved. Public expenditure is thus the only legitimate way that governments have to implement their policies. It is in the outlay of expenditure and revenue measures that priorities can be seen. In order to promote employment, governments may introduce public works for a variety of purposes, for example, construction of roads, housing, health and education services. In its decisions regarding priorities, it may decide to spend more on education so as to build future human capital. Or a country may decide to carry out mandatory HIV testing for its citizens, given the unrelenting scale of the AIDS pandemic.

In designing effective development policies, it is all about choices, choices, choices and money, money, money. But what are the real results? Are they enhancing the achievement of rights and therefore the true freedoms that lead to genuine human development? This is certainly an area to watch in the struggle for all human rights for all people. It is also a challenge because it is one area that is prone to capture by unaccountable politicians, and misuse by civil servants, in an impoverished country.

5. Investment in Education

The returns on investment in education are multiple and can be long-lasting. Better health and entrepreneurship and social engagement are some of these returns. Developing countries, especially in Africa, have often succumbed to a donor emphasis that focuses on primary education without building the next levels of education, secondary and tertiary.

In Zambia for instance whilst primary schooling is widespread, only a half of the eligible population is in secondary school and less than a quarter make it to tertiary. The quality of primary education has become poorer over the years. This is a cycle that has to be broken. An educated populace is more able to engage in social accountability initiatives, is more able to fight for its rights, is more able to question its leaders. Paul VI's views are very clear and cogent:

> It can even be affirmed that economic growth depends in the very first place upon social progress: thus basic education is the primary object of any plan of development. Indeed hunger for education is no less debasing than hunger for food: an illiterate is a person with an undernourished mind. To be able to read and write, to acquire a professional formation, means to recover confidence in oneself and to discover that one can progress along with the others (n. 35).

Conclusion

Human rights are indeed a development challenge. That is the message I want to convey in this reflection on one aspect of the promotion of integral and sustainable human development. The message of *Populorum Progressio* is still as valid today as it was 40 years ago:

Freedom from misery, the greater assurance of finding subsistence, health and fixed employment; an increased share of responsibility without oppression of any kind and in security from situations that do violence to their dignity as men; better education – in brief, to seek to do more, know more and have more in order to be more: that is what men aspire to now when a greater number of them are condemned to live in conditions that make this lawful desire illusory. Besides, peoples who have recently gained national independence experience the need to add to this political freedom a fitting autonomous growth, social as well as economic, in order to assure their citizens of a full human enhancement and to take their rightful place with other nations (n. 6).

References

Sen, Amartya (1999), *Development as Freedom*, Oxford: Oxford University Press.

UNDP (2000), *Human Development Report*, New York: Oxford University Press.

Migration and the Development of Peoples

Eugene Quinn

Introduction

International migration is not a new phenomenon. For centuries, people have crossed national borders in search of better lives and to escape from war and conflict, hunger and poverty, demographic pressures and resource depletion.

Globalisation has ushered in a new era of mobility. The magnitude and complexity of international migration makes it an important force in development and a high-priority issue for both developing and developed countries. 'Migration is increasingly being perceived as a development tool. It is no longer seen as a failure of development, but rather as an integral aspect of the global development process' (Obaid, 2004). However, migration remains a controversial and divisive issue both in domestic and international arenas, although the positive dimensions are increasingly recognised.

Kofi Annan, the former United Nations Secretary General, has described migration as 'a courageous expression of an individual's will to overcome adversity and live a better life'. He has talked about how governments can play a role in creating triple wins – for migrants, for countries of origin and for host societies (Annan, 2006). The funds migrants send to their home countries as remittances amounted to $167 billion in 2005, dwarfing the total international development aid donated in that year. The demographic trends in developed countries mean that they will require significant inflows of migrant workers to sustain their economies. However, the size and diversity of migrant flows have given rise to new challenges for their countries of origin, which find themselves deprived of many of what are often seen as their 'brightest and best'. There are also challenges for the countries of destination, which have to deal with the complex issues of integration, xenophobia, human trafficking and migrant rights.

The Facts about Migration

Three per cent of the world's people live outside their country of origin. International migrants numbered 191 million in 2005, with 115 million living in developed countries. About a third of all migrants moved from one developing country to another and another third from a developing country to a developed country. Thus, 'South-South' migration is as significant as 'South-North' migration.

Economic migrants are the world's fastest growing group of migrants. The International Labour Organisation (ILO) estimates that about half of all international migrants (that is, around 95 million) are in the labour force. This is the totality of migrants who work, irrespective of their admission or legal status.

The United Nations Population Fund estimates there are 30 to 40 million people worldwide who have migrated without proper authorisation. The US hosts just over 10 million undocumented migrants, and around half a million arrive each year. By comparison, there is somewhere between seven and eight million in Europe. Undocumented migrants often face dangerous journeys, exploitation by criminal smuggling networks, difficult working and living conditions, and intolerance when they arrive on foreign soil.

In addition to those who migrate for work and better opportunities, there are the significant numbers of people who leave their own country to seek asylum. At the beginning of 2006, there were, according to the United Nations High Commissioner for Refugees (UNHCR), 773,500 asylum seekers and 8.4 million refugees worldwide. In addition, there were 2.4 million stateless people. Along with the more than 11 million people in these categories, there were 6.6 million 'internally displaced' people (people caught in situations similar to refugees, but who have stayed in their own countries rather than cross an international frontier); 1.6 million 'returned refugees', and 960,400 who were otherwise 'of concern' to the UNHCR. In total, then, the total number of 'people of concern' to the UNHCR in 2006 was 20.8 million (UNHCR, 2006).

Women, once considered passive players who accompanied or

joined migrating husbands or other family members, are play-ing an increasing role in international migration. Pope Benedict XVI (2006) in his Message for World Day of Migrants and Refugees drew attention to the growing 'feminisation' of migra-tion: women now constitute nearly half of the migrant popul-ation worldwide and between 70 and 80 per cent of the migrant population in some countries. Because women migrants often work in unregulated sectors of the economy, they are at a much higher risk of violence, human trafficking and sexual abuse. Therefore, the gender dimensions of migration deserve in-creased attention.

'Push' and 'Pull' Factors

The Widening Gap

'Every hour more than 1,200 children die away from the glare of media attention. This is the equivalent of three tsunamis a month, every month, hitting the world's most vulnerable citi-zens – its children. The causes of death will vary, but the over-whelming majority can be traced to a single pathology: poverty.' (UNDP, 2006, 1) So opens the *Human Development Report* 2005. The report highlights the growing gulf between those who 'have', the one fifth of humanity that thinks nothing of spending $2 on a cappuccino, and those who 'have-not', the one fifth of humanity that survives on less than a dollar a day (UNDP, 2006, 3). The Jesuit theologian, Jon Sobrino, describes this situation where more than a billion people on the planet live on less than a dollar a day as a 'macro-blasphemy'.

Often at the root of forced migration is a world economic system that does not work. Income inequalities between the developed and developing worlds are stark. A consequence of globalis-ation is that, through television, films, the internet and the ever-expanding means of global communication, the world's poorest peoples are increasingly aware of how the other half lives. The widening gap between rich and poor countries has led many people to vote with their feet, leaving their homelands in search of a better life for themselves and their families.

Systemic faults in global economic and governance structures have, in the case of many developing countries, led to a failure to eradicate abject poverty, created fertile conditions for war and conflict and through widespread environmental degradation exacerbated natural disasters. The absence of international solidarity has allowed a situation to develop where many of the world's most vulnerable citizens are forced to leave their countries, their families and their homes. In *Populorum Progressio*, Pope Paul VI warned that unless action is taken, the disparity between rich and poor nations will increase rather than diminish (n. 8).

Conflict
Conflict, persecution and violence force millions of people worldwide to leave their homes and to seek refuge in other nations. Many of the people forcibly displaced by war and conflict find themselves in camps in neighbouring countries or regions, living in cramped and hazardous conditions. The roots of conflicts can often be traced back to exaggerated nationalism (Yugoslavia) and, in many countries, to hatred and systematic or violent exclusion of ethnic or religious minorities from society (Rwanda).

Research commissioned by the World Bank, and published as *Breaking the Conflict Trap* (Collier et al, 2003), has shown that the combination of poverty, economic decline and dependence on exporting natural resources drives conflict across all regions. Many of the poorest countries are locked in a vicious circle in which poverty causes conflict and conflict causes poverty. The report showed that the incidence of civil war globally had risen over the previous forty years and that sixteen of the twenty poorest countries in the world had suffered a major civil war in the previous fifteen years.

The report's analysis of 52 major civil wars that occurred between 1960 and 1999 showed that:
- The typical conflict had lasted about seven years and had left the country in which it occurred poor and disease-ridden.
- Countries coming out of war faced a 50 per cent chance of relapsing in the first five years of peace.
- Even with rapid progress after peace, it can take a generation or more just to return to pre-war living standards.

In *Populorum Progressio*, Paul VI argues that peace is more than just the absence of warfare. He emphasises the connection between poverty and conflict, and – as has been mentioned elsewhere in this volume – proclaims that development is 'the new name for peace' (n. 87).

Demographic Trends

In many developed nations, particularly in Europe and parts of Asia, population decline, largely the result of below-replacement fertility, and population ageing, have emerged as significant concerns and their effects are expected to grow in the future. Currently, developed countries have 142 potential entrants into the labour force for every 100 persons expected to retire. In just 10 years, however, this ratio will drop to 87 new entrants per 100 pending retirees (Sutherland, 2006).

Advanced economies will therefore soon have a large deficit of workers relative both to the jobs that need to be filled, and to the taxes that need to be generated. If this situation continues, it will threaten developed countries' ability to sustain economic growth and to maintain their existing pension and social security systems.

The population crisis of developed countries creates a compelling 'pull' factor for migrants, given that developing countries have a labour replacement ratio of 342 persons per 100 retirees, an excess that is expected to eventually decline but that will continue for the foreseeable future (Sutherland, 2006). Migration therefore has taken on an increased significance for developed countries and for them has become a key component of population growth and labour market supply.

Natural and Environmental Disasters

Mass migration often results from natural phenomena such as earthquakes, volcanic eruptions and hurricanes. These events cause flooding, destroy housing and disrupt agriculture, making it difficult or impossible for inhabitants to stay within their communities. The Asian tsunami of December 2004, for example, wreaked a terrifying trail of destruction and havoc resulting in the death of thousands and the displacement of millions.

Large-scale industrial and nuclear accidents, such as those that occurred in Bhopal and Chernobyl, have long-term conse-quences. One is that thousands of people may be forced from their homes, often with little or no hope of return. Other human-created environmental problems, such as global warming, pol-lution of rivers, soil erosion and desertification, lead to a more gradual displacement of people.

Benefits and Costs of Migration

Benefits

There is a growing awareness of the ways in which migrants can help transform their adopted and their native countries. Migration can play a positive role by providing the workers to satisfy the labour demands of advanced economies and of dy-namic developing economies, while at the same time reducing unemployment and underemployment in countries of origin. 'By enlarging the labour force and the pool of consumers and by contributing their entrepreneurial capacities, migrants boost economic growth in receiving countries' (United Nations, 2006, 13). For example, research has shown that migrants have con-tributed positively to economic growth in Ireland, and have alle-viated both skills and labour shortages (National Economic and Social Council, 2006, 71).

Remittances are the most immediate and tangible benefit of in-ternational migration. In many developing countries, remit-tances received from migrants constitute a more important source of income than either Official Development Assistance (ODA) or Foreign Direct Investment (FDI). The World Bank esti-mates that, at the world level, remittances transfers more than doubled between 1995 and 2005, rising from $102 billion to an estimated $232 billion. The share of global remittances received by developing countries has also increased, from 57 per cent in 1995 ($58 billion) to 72 per cent in 2005 ($165 billion) (UN, 2006, 54).

Even though sub-Saharan Africa receives the lowest proportion of remittances of all developing regions, transfers from migrants still have a very significant impact there. Household incomes in Somalia, for example, are doubled by remittances, while finan-cial transfers provide 80 per cent of the income of rural households in Lesotho (Global Commission on International Migration, 2005, 27).

Countries of origin expect that the highly trained returnees will contribute to the transfer of knowledge and technology needed to grow their economies, facilitate institution-building and accelerate economic growth,

> Migrants themselves through their action of leaving do contribute to development and poverty reduction. It is accomplished through the reinvestment of their skills, if and when they return, but also through the investment of their remittances, which are sent to relatives and which are at times directly reinvested in the economy. (Di Marzio, 2006)

Costs

No one can deny that international migration has negative aspects – trafficking, smuggling, social discontent – or that it often arises from poverty or political strife. Border and immigration controls are costly for states to administer. This has become even more so due to increased threats to national security from international terrorism.

One of the most insidious developments has been the growth in trafficking of human persons for purposes of forced labour and prostitution. Pope Benedict XVI has pointed out that trafficking in human beings, especially women 'flourishes where opportunities to improve their standard of living or even to survive is limited'. He connects this aspect of migration to the commercial sex industry, condemning 'the widespread hedonistic and commercial culture which encourages the systematic exploitation of sexuality' (Pope Benedict XVI, 2006).

Displacement of local workers by lower-paid migrants is a fear often articulated by trade unions in developed countries. There has been much debate about whether migrants compete with or complement native workers, but empirical research shows that, although migrants may cause some reduction in wages, or higher unemployment among low-skilled native workers and among previous migrants, these effects are very small and are certainly less than the positive effects migration has in promoting additional demand for goods and services and hence economic growth (United Nations, 2006, 22).

International cooperation has often focused on keeping migrants out rather than seeking ways to effectively integrate them into host societies. Heightened concerns regarding international terrorism and national security after 9/11 have created a more hostile environment for migrants, particularly asylum seekers, many of whom are travelling on no or false travel documents. In the European Union, internal barriers to movement of peoples have been removed while external borders have been strengthened, leading to accusations that a 'Fortress Europe' is being created.

The precarious situation of so many migrants, which should arouse solidarity, instead sometimes gives rise to hostility in certain sections of host societies, who feel that immigrants are a burden, regard them with suspicion and even consider them a danger and a threat. This often provokes intolerance, xenophobia, racism and at times violence. Politically this fear may be manifested in a rise in support for anti-immigrant parties of the Far Right.

Isolation and marginalisation of migrants and new communities may lead to anger and discontent, which may find expression in crime, dangerous fundamentalism and hostility towards state authorities. The street riots in France during 2006 highlighted the failure to provide effective employment, housing, education and other social policies necessary to ensure integration.

Migration Challenges and Church Teaching

The Right Not to Have to Emigrate

Building on the idea, advanced by Paul VI, that 'development is the new name for peace', Pope John Paul II (2004) in his Message for World Day of Migrants and Refugees, stated:

> ... building conditions of peace means in practice being seriously committed to safeguarding first of all the right not to emigrate, that is, the right to live in peace and dignity in one's own country. By means of a farsighted local and national administration, more equitable trade and supportive international cooperation, it is possible for every country to guarantee its own population, in addition to freedom of expression and movement, the possibility to satisfy basic needs such as food, health care, work, housing and education; the frustration of these needs forces many into a position where their only option is to emigrate.

People should have the opportunity to remain in their home-land to support and to find full lives for themselves and their families. This is the ideal situation for which the international community must strive: one in which migration flows are driven by choice, not necessity.

Migrants also want the chance to return home if conditions have improved. The Jesuit Refugee Service has advocated that equal attention be given to creating an environment in the countries and regions of origin from where the forcibly displaced come that will allow sustainable development to occur. The forcibly displaced are usually unwilling to return if it is not safe for them to do so, or if they are unsure that their human rights will be respected. Nor are they willing to return if they feel that they will not be able to provide for themselves or their families, or if they will not have access to basic health care and education (Jesuit Refugee Service, 2006).

Rights of Migrant Workers
Often migrant workers are deprived of their most basic human rights. Church teaching emphasises that migrant workers are not to be considered as just another factor of production: every migrant enjoys inalienable fundamental rights that must be respected.

Church documents have repeatedly called for the ratification by states of the International Convention on the Protection of the Rights of All Migrant Workers and the Members of their Families, seeing the Convention as a framework for safeguarding the rights of migrant workers. The European Platform for Migrant Workers' Rights (2005) has described the main features of the Convention as follows:

- Migrant workers are viewed as more than labourers or economic entities. They are social entities with families and accordingly have rights, including that of family reunification.
- The Convention recognises that migrant workers and members of their families, being non-nationals residing in states of employment or in transit, often find themselves in a situation lacking the protection of their basic human rights.

- The Convention provides an international definition of 'migrant worker' and it establishes international standards of treatment through the elaboration of the particular human rights of migrant workers and members of their families.
- Fundamental rights are extended to all migrant workers, both documented and undocumented, with additional rights being recognised for documented migrant workers and members of their families, notably equality of treatment with nationals of states of employment in a number of legal, political, economic, social and cultural areas.
- The Convention seeks to play a role in preventing and eliminating the exploitation of all migrant workers and members of their families, including ending their illegal or clandestine movements and irregular or undocumented situations.

Irregular Migration

Irregular migration is often a highly contentious aspect of international migration. The Global Commission on International Migration noted that an individual person cannot be 'irregular' or 'illegal', and therefore in its report adopted the term 'migrants with irregular status'. The Commission included in this category migrants who enter or remain in a country without authorisation, those who are smuggled or trafficked across an international border, unsuccessful asylum seekers who fail to observe a deportation order and people who circumvent immigration controls through the arrangement of bogus marriages (Global Commission on International Migration, 2005, 32).

The International Centre on Migration Policy Development estimates that some 2,000 migrants die each year while trying to cross the Mediterranean from Africa to Europe. Furthermore, about 400 Mexicans die each year while attempting to cross the border into the United States (GCIM, 2005, 34). As a result of the conditions under which they have to travel – arising from arrangements made by smugglers who demand large sums of money for their 'services' – many migrants have drowned at sea, suffocated in sealed containers or been assaulted while in transit.

Even if migrants with irregular status are lucky enough to survive the journey, their rights tend to be highly restricted by host states. The fear of deportation often means that they will not access even the limited public services to which they may be entitled. The vulnerability of their situation leaves them open to further exploitation and abuse.

What drives migrants to take such a desperate gamble? At the root of this phenomenon is invariably poverty and lack of opportunity. In the absence of any prospects at home, such migrants are prepared to take enormous risks in the belief and hope that moving to a developed country will bring the chance of a better life for themselves and their families.

It is clear that states have a right to control their borders. International terrorism, crime, illegal drugs and smuggling are some of the threats to national security that result in countries policing their borders ever more vigilantly. Church teaching recognises the sovereign right of nations to determine who enters and who remains. However, states must also protect the rights of migrants with irregular status. Furthermore, states must ensure that the internationally agreed right to seek asylum under the Geneva Convention is not undermined by excessively restrictive and stringent immigration procedures.

The Jesuit Refugee Service (JRS) Europe has challenged the widespread practice of detaining asylum seekers entering EU Member States. In its report, *Detention in Europe*, JRS acknowledges the concern of states with regard to security, especially following 11 September 2001 and 11 March 2004 (the Madrid bombings). However, it argues that any necessary safeguards should not be used as a pretext to detain asylum seekers and immigrants. Criminal and administrative law can and should address the problem of threats to national security and public order. It is therefore unnecessary to criminalise innocent refugees and migrants through restrictive administrative practices such as detention (Jesuit Refugee Service, Europe, 2004).

Brain Drain

A recurring concern is that migration robs developing nations of their 'brightest and best' and that this loss of human capital seriously undermines development. The phenomenon of the most educated people leaving a developing country in search of better economic conditions is often termed 'brain drain'. The Global Commission on International Migration sees the notion of 'brain drain' as outmoded.

> In the current era, there is a need to capitalise upon the growth of human mobility by promoting the notion of 'brain circulation', in which migrants return to their own country on a regular or occasional basis, sharing the benefits of the skills and resources they have acquired while living and working abroad.
> (Global Commission on Migration, 2005, 31)

Nonetheless, it is necessary to recognise the potential negative impact of the migration of skilled personnel from developing countries. Particular concern relates to the health care sector where the Western world's shortage of nurses has resulted in the recruitment of thousands of trained nurses from developing countries which themselves desperately need to build up their health services (Bosch, Bou and Haddad, 2006, 166). Some of the adverse effects of the 'brain drain' can be mitigated through international cooperation – for example, compensating developing countries for loss of skilled personnel or paying for training.

Avoiding Discrimination and Promoting Integration
Public resentment of migrants and fear of difference can lead to discrimination, community tensions, and occasional violence. In addition, they can contribute to the rise in support for far-right political parties, which successfully exploit people's fears and resentments.

Difference in religious beliefs between migrants and host societies may also give rise to tensions. For instance, the growth, largely as a result of migration, of the Muslim population in the countries of the European Union – currently some 20 million in a population of 450 million EU citizens and increasing fast – has highlighted the differences between conservative Islamic values and Europe's secular liberalism. The demographic shift, assimilation difficulties, and debates over issues such as head scarves and the role of women in society have occasionally sparked violent disagreements. Concerns about terrorism – arising especially from the March 2004 bombings in Madrid and the July 2005 bombings in London – and incidents like the November 2004 murder of Dutch filmmaker Theo van Gogh, have forced countries to reconsider how to handle their rapidly growing Muslim communities. All these factors point to the need for a comprehensive integration strategy.

Pope John Paul II addressed the issue of integration in successive Messages for World Day for Migrants and Refugees. In the 2004 Message, for example, he stated:

> If the gradual integration of all immigrants is fostered with respect for their identity and, at the same time, safeguarding the cultural patrimony of the peoples who receive them, there is less of a risk that they will come together to form real 'ghettos' in which they remain isolated from the social context. (Pope John Paul II, 2004)

And in his 2005 Message, John Paul said:

> The way to take is the path of genuine integration with an open outlook that refuses to consider solely the differences between immigrants and the local people. Thus the need for a dialogue between people of different cultures in a context of pluralism that goes beyond mere tolerance and reaches sympathy. (Pope John Paul II, 2005)

In the 2005 Message, he also addressed the issue of inter-religious dialogue. He called on Christians to recognise in the various cultures of new communities the presence of 'precious elements of religion and humanity' that can offer solid prospects of mutual understanding. He added: 'It will, of course, be necessary to combine the respect for cultural differences with the protection of values that are common and inalienable, because they are founded on human rights' (Pope John Paul II, 2005).

Principles of Church Social Teaching

In 2003 the Catholic Bishops Conferences of the Unites States and Mexico issued a joint Pastoral Letter concerning migration (*Strangers no Longer*, 2003). The Bishops enunciated five principles, derived from the tradition of church teachings with regard to migration, which should guide migration policy:

I. *Persons have the right to find opportunities in their homeland*
   All persons have the right to find in their own countries the economic, political, and social opportunities to live in dignity and achieve a full life through the use of their

God-given gifts. In this context, work that provides a just, living wage is a basic human need.

II. *Persons have the right to migrate to support themselves and their families*

The church recognises that all the goods of the earth belong to all people. When persons cannot find employment in their country of origin to support themselves and their families, they have a right to find work elsewhere in order to survive. Sovereign nations should provide ways to accommodate this right.

III. *Sovereign nations have the right to control their borders*

The church recognises the right of sovereign nations to control their territories but rejects such control when it is exerted merely for the purpose of acquiring additional wealth. More powerful economic nations, which have the ability to protect and feed their residents, have a stronger obligation to accommodate migration flows.

IV. *Refugees and asylum seekers should be afforded protection*

Those who flee wars and persecution should be protected by the global community. This requires, at a minimum, that migrants have a right to claim refugee status without incarceration and to have their claims fully considered by a competent authority.

V. *The human dignity and human rights of undocumented migrants should be respected*

Regardless of their legal status, migrants, like all persons, possess inherent human dignity that should be respected. Often they are subject to punitive laws and harsh treatment from enforcement officers from both receiving and transit countries. Government policies that respect the basic human rights of the undocumented are necessary.

Migration and Solidarity

At the heart of the Christian response to the situation of migrants in the world today is the challenge of solidarity, one of the fundamental principles of Catholic social teaching. Solidarity, in this understanding, goes beyond a 'feeling of vague compassion, or shallow distress at the misfortunes of so many people, both near or far' and calls for 'a firm and persevering determination to commit oneself to the common good; that is to say, to the good of all and of each individual because we are all really responsible for all' (Pope John Paul II, 1987).

For both individuals and societies, making real the principle of solidarity in our response to international migration is not an easy task, given the complexity of the issue and the many different dimensions involved: economic demands, security considerations, social integration, cultural diversity, religion. Above all, however, as the Pontifical Council for the Pastoral Care of Migrants and Itinerant People (2004) has noted: 'migration raises a truly ethical question: the search for a new international economic order for a more equitable distribution of the goods of the earth' (*Erga Migrantes Caritas Christi*, n. 8).

It is in answering this question, which inextricably links migration and development, that we are called to build a world '...where all people, no matter what their race, religion or nationality, can live fully human lives, freed from servitude imposed on them by others or by natural forces over which they have not sufficient control; a world where freedom is not an empty word' (*Populorum Progressio*, n. 47).

References
Annan, Kofi (2006) *The Secretary-General Address to the High-Level Dialogue of the General Assembly on International Migration and Development*, New York, 14 September 2006. Available: http://www.un.org/migration/sg-speech.html (Accessed 8 January 2007).

Bosch, Peter, Jean-Pierre Bou & Emma Haddad (2006) 'The Opportunities and Challenges of Migration' in Jesuit Centre for Faith and Justice, *The Future of Europe: Uniting Vision, Values and Citizens*, Dublin: Veritas.

Collier, Paul *et al* (2003) *Breaking the Conflict Trap: Civil War and Development Policy*, Washington DC: World Bank and New York: Oxford University Press.

Committee on Migration of the United States Conference of Catholic Bishops and the Conferencia del Episcopado Mexicano (2003) *Strangers No Longer: Together on the Journey of Hope, A Pastoral Letter Concerning Migration from the Catholic Bishops of Mexico and the United States.*

European Platform for Migrant Workers Rights (2005) *EPMWR –*

Comments on the Green Paper on Economic Migration. Available: http://www.december18.net/ (Accessed 24 January 2007).

Di Marzio, Nicholas (2006) 'Challenges for the Future of Global Migration', Paper to 54th Council Meeting of the International Catholic Migration Commission, Rome, 3 July 2006.

Global Commission on International Migration (2005) *Migration in an Interconnected World: New Directions for Action,* Geneva: Global Commission on International Migration. Available: http://www.gcim.org/ (Accessed 8 January 2007).

Jesuit Refugee Service (2006) JRS Position on Migration and Development for the High Level Dialogue on Migration Development at the United Nation, 14–16 September, 2006. Available: http://www.jrseurope.org/ (Accessed 26 January 2007).

Jesuit Refugee Service Europe (2004) *Detention in Europe, Observation and Position Document,* Brussels: JRS Europe.

National Economic and Social Council (2006) *Managing Migration in Ireland: A Social and Economic Analysis, A Report by the International Organization for Migration for the National Economic and Social Council of Ireland,* Dublin: National Economic and Social Development Office.

Obaid, Thoraya Ahmed (2004) *Round Table on International Migration and Development: The Challenges Ahead,* Available: http://www.unfpa.org/ (Accessed 4 January 2007).

Pontifical Council for the Pastoral Care of Migrants and Itinerant People (2004) *Erga Migrantes Caritas Christi* (The Love of Christ towards Migrants), Vatican City.

Pope Benedict XVI (2006) *Migration: a Sign of the Times,* Message for World Day of Migrants and Refugees 2006. Available: http://www.vatican.va/holy_father/benedict_xvi/messages/migration/ (Accessed 14 January 2007).

Pope John Paul II (1987) *Solicitudo Rei Socialis* (The Social Concern of the Church), Encyclical Letter, 30 December 1987, London: Catholic Truth Society.

Pope John Paul II (2004) *Migration with a View to Peace,* Message for World Day of Migrants and Refugees 2004. Available: http://www.vatican.va/holy_father/john_paul_ii/messages/migration/ (Accessed 14 January 2007).

Pope John Paul II (2005) *Intercultural Integration,* Message for World Day of Migrants and Refugees 2005. Available: http://www.vatican.va/holy_father/john_paul_ii/messages/migration/ (Accessed 14 January 2007).

Pope Paul VI (1967) *Populorum Progressio* (The Development of

Peoples), Encyclical Letter, 26 March 1967, London: Catholic Truth Society.

Sutherland, Peter (2006) 'Migration and Development', Presentation to Conference 'Ireland and Global Development: Strengthening Financial, Trade and Health Systems', Trinity College Dublin, 5–6 July 2006. Available: http://www.tcd.ie/iiis/pages/events/irlglobalde-vschedule.php (Accessed 15 January 2007).

United Nations (2006) *International Migration and Development: Report of the Secretary General* (A/60/871). Available: http://www.un.org/esa/population/migration/hld/index.html (Accessed 4 January 2007).

United Nations Development Programme (2006) *Human Development Report 2005: International Cooperation at a Crossroads, Aid, Trade and Security in an Unequal World*, New York: United Nations Development Programme.

United Nations High Commissioner for Refugees (2006) *Refugee by Numbers: 2006 Edition*, Geneva: United Nations High Commissioner for Refugees.

The Lack of an Ecological Critique in Catholic Social Teaching

Seán McDonagh SSC

Much of the teaching in *Populorum Progressio* is as relevant today as when it was written. However it is completely silent on one of the most central challenges of our time – the massive and often irreversible destruction of the environment. A key problem arises from the fact that the encyclical is totally human-centred. For instance the encyclical states: 'In the very first pages of scripture we read these words: "Fill the earth and subdue it."' This teaches us that the whole of creation is for man, that he has been charged to give it meaning by his intelligent activity, to complete and perfect it by his own efforts and to his own advantage (*Populorum Progressio*, n. 22).

According to the above, the earth and other creatures have no intrinsic value. All they have is instrumental value in so far as they serve human needs. This is further reflected in the same section of the document referred to above:

> Now if the earth truly was created to provide man with the necessities of life and the tools for his own progress, it follows that every man has the right to glean what he needs from the earth. The recent Council reiterated this truth: God intended the earth and everything in it for the use of all human beings and peoples. Thus, under the leadership of justice and in the company of charity, created goods should flow fairly to all. (n. 22)

This homocentric focus in Catholic social teaching is not based on a biblical understanding of creation but rather on the thoughts of the Greek philosopher Protagoras who was born in Abdera around 481 BCE. His axiom that 'man is the measure of all things: of things which are, that they are so, and of things which are not, that they are not', has had a profound impact on Western culture, especially since the Enlightenment. We are not actually sure what Protagoras himself meant by the statement. In recent centuries, it has been understood as a proud assertion of human pre-eminence over all creation, a distancing of the human from the rest of creation and a claim that all creation was there primarily for the benefit of humankind.

This philosophy has gained almost infallible status in Catholic thinking and is still very much in place. For example, Vatican II is undoubtedly the major achievement of the Catholic Church in the 20th century. *Gaudium et Spes* (the Constitution of the Church in the Modern World) is a milestone in the history of the church's attitude towards the world. It embodies a positive, liberating vision of life that refuses to seal off the religious world from the rest of human affairs. One cannot, however, argue that it is grounded in an ecological vision of reality. This document subscribes to what is called a 'domination theology'. The natural world is there for man's exclusive use, 'for man, created in God's image, received a mandate to subject to himself all that it contains, and govern the world with justice and holiness' (*Gaudium et Spes* n. 34).

Populorum Progressio shows no sensitivity to the ecological issue. Significantly, the document contains no caution about the impact of industrialisation on the biosphere. It states boldly that, 'the introduction of industry is necessary for economic growth and human progress; it is also a sign of development and contributes to it. By persistent work and the use of his intelligence man gradually wrests nature's secrets from her and finds a better application for her riches' (n. 25).

Yet, as one phase of the industrial revolution followed another the dark side of technology began to appear. This includes global warming and climate change, the depletion of the ozone region, the destruction of biodiversity, acid rain, soil erosion, pollution of oceans and rivers and nuclear waste. The encyclical and much of subsequent Catholic social teaching is silent on all of this.

The Fathers of the Vatican Council and the drafters of *Populorum Progressio* cannot claim that there was no understanding of environmental damage in the 1960s. The Council opened in October 1962. In April of the same year Rachel Carson published her ground-breaking book *Silent Spring*. This book is often seen as marking the beginning of the modern ecological movement. The book challenged and dismantled the claims of the chemical industry that pesticides, especially organochlorines, were harmless. Carson used science and case studies to show the gruesome details of acute poisoning of human, vegetation and wildlife that resulted from the insect control programmes. Her three books on the oceans – *Under the Sea-Wind, The Sea around Us,* and *The Edge of the Sea* – are awe-inspiring. They challenge our propensity to view nature always from an anthropocentric point of view. For Carson, humans are only one strand in the web of life and not everything on earth is there for our use and gratification.

Climate Change

Climate change is the most important issue facing the planet and therefore humanity at this moment. Humans have lived for the past 11,000 years in pretty stable and predictable climatic conditions. This, for example, made farming and larger-scale human settlements possible. Now, with the rise of greenhouse gases, mainly carbon dioxide, in the atmosphere we are changing the climate of the planet in a major way. Before the beginning of the industrial revolution there were 280 parts per million (ppm) of carbon dioxide or its equivalent in the air. It is now 450 ppm of carbon dioxide or of carbon equivalent such as methane and the level is rising fast. If we continue in a business-as-usual fashion we will have reached 550 ppm by the middle of this century. The last time this happened in the history of the planet was during the Eocene period, 50 million years ago. At that time it was warm at the North Pole and sea-levels were three hundred feet higher than they are today.

As we can see, climate change is happening quite suddenly. The US scientist Richard Alley is quoted recently as saying: 'We used to think that it would take 10,000 years for melting at the surface of an ice sheet to penetrate down to the bottom. Now we know that it doesn't take 10,000 years; it takes 10 seconds' (quoted in Pearce, 2006, p. 8). Given the seriousness of this situation for every succeeding generation on the planet, how have the churches responded to date to this immense crisis?

Over the years the World Council of Churches has developed an extensive body of teaching on global warming. This includes a document published in May 1994 called *Sign of Peril, Test of Faith, Accelerated Climate Change,* and more recently in 2002 a pamphlet, *Solidarity with Victims of Climate Change* (World Council of Churches, 1994; 2002). In March 1996 the then President of the Pontifical Council for Justice and Peace, Cardinal Roger Etchegaray, wrote to the Presidents of the Episcopal Conferences of industrial countries and acknowledged that the World Council of Churches has 'taken a leading role in drawing the attention of its member churches to the relationship between climate change and human activity'. He encouraged local churches to examine ways in which they could co-operate with any WCC-inspired initiative in their country. Unfortunately, little happened then or is happening now.

In 2002, the WCC followed up with another excellent document on climate change entitled *Solidarity with Victims of Climate Change*. This document pointed out that the extreme weather conditions caused by climate change are costing a fortune. Insurance companies claim that very soon the bill will mount up to $300 billion annually. Countries in the majority world will be the most vulnerable. The document recognises that the Kyoto Protocol is only a beginning because the scientists on the Intergovernmental Panel on Climate Change (IPCC) were calling for a 60 per cent to 80 per cent reduction in greenhouse gas emissions by the year 2050 whereas the reduction for industrialised countries in the protocol has only reached 5.2 per cent. The document does point out that, with the vast array of technologies and policy measures on energy supply and demand, the targets are achievable if there is strong political leadership (World Council of Churches, 2002, p. 11).

On pages 13 and 14 the document discusses the World Trade Organisation (WTO) Conference in Doha (November 2001). They make the valid point that it is almost impossible to insert binding ecological criteria into the workings of the WTO: 'The system is basically incapable of integrating the environmental dimension. Though market mechanisms are to be affirmed for the promotion of the exchange of goods, they are unable to set the scales and limits which must be respected for the sake of the environment. For measures containing the dynamism of the market the role of the state is indispensable' (World Council of Churches, 2002, p. 14).

The WCC 2002 document is an accurate and bleak assessment of the current ecological situation. It states that 'destructive processes have continued and are continuing. Change is unlikely to occur through persuasion. It may take place as the dysfunctioning of the system becomes more and more obvious. It will be accompanied by upheavals and suffering.' The pamphlet ends with a brief theological reflection that is very appropriate in the current context. 'There is no guarantee that resistance will be crowned by success. The future is unknown. There is a distinct possibility that "love will grow cold" (Mt 24:12). It is essential that our love does not depend on the assurances of success. Faith, hope and love abide, says Paul. Love transcends the limits of this life. The hope for God's absolute future is the ultimate motivation of love' (WCC, 2002, p. 26).

The Catholic Church
In contrast to the WCC response to this and other ecological issues, Catholic teaching on global warming, either from the papal magisterium or bishops' conferences, is pretty meagre. In 2002, Sister Marjorie Keenan wrote a book drawing together papal teaching on the ecologist crisis (Keenan, 2002). While she has done an excellent job in bringing this teaching together in a single volume, it is still a rather slim one. If one were to bring together the recent teachings on sexual matters within the Catholic Church, I think it would be a much heftier set of volumes!

One of the first places where there is a reference to global warming in papal teaching is in the 1990 document on ecology: *Peace with God the Creator; Peace with all Creation*. The sixth paragraph of the document lumps together global warming and the destruction of the ozone layer by chlorofluorocarbons (CFCs). The documents states that 'The gradual depletion of the ozone layer and the related "greenhouse effect" have now reached crisis proportions...'. While CFCs are global warming gases, the depletion of the ozone layer and global warming are two different things. This, of course, underscores the need for moral teaching on any ecological issues to be grounded in accurate science.

There is a brief mention of global warming in the newly published *Compendium of the Social Doctrine of the Church* (2004). N. 470 of the *Compendium* states:

Every economic activity making use of natural resources must also be concerned with safeguarding the environment and should foresee the costs involved, which are an essential part of the actual cost of economic activity. In this context, *one considers relations between human activity and climate change which, given their extreme complexity, must be opportunely and constantly monitored at the scientific, political and juridical, national and international levels. The climate is a good that must be protected* and reminds consumers and those engaged in industrial activity to develop a greater sense of responsibility for their behaviour. [Emphasis added]

There is little sense in this quotation of the magnitude of this problem and the urgency with which it must be faced, given the fact that global warming is probably the most serious problem facing the planet and humanity and that action on fossil fuel emission is urgent if we are to avert the worse case scenarios for the planet and humankind.

Climate Change and Common Good

Thus far the leadership of the Catholic Church, globally and in Ireland, has failed to give effective guidance on the most important challenge facing humanity and the planet, namely the environmental crisis. The tragedy is made even more poignant by the fact that there are plenty of resources within the Catholic tradition to give robust leadership in this area.

The *Compendium* states that 'climate is a good that must be protected'. Concern for the 'common good' has traditionally been at the heart of Catholic moral and social teaching. In an extensive reflection on the 'common good' the *Compendium* goes on to state that: 'the common good that people seek and attain in the formation of social communities is the guarantee of their personal, familial and associative good' (nn. 61, 164, 165, 168, 170). What the *Compendium*, with the exception of n. 170, and almost all Catholic social teaching overlooks, is that life-giving human social relations are always embedded in vibrant and sustainable ecosystems. Anything that negatively impacts on ecosystems or alters the equilibrium of the biosphere, such as global warming, is a disruption of the common good in a most fundamental way – especially if it creates negative irreversible changes. This is exactly what climate change is doing. To sum up the challenge briefly: in January 2004, Sir David King, the chief scientist to the

British Government, stated that climate change was the most serious issue facing the human community. Therefore in his view, US climate policy is a bigger threat to the world than terrorism is. 'As a consequence of continued warming, millions more people around the world may in future be exposed to the risk of hunger, drought, flooding and debilitating diseases such as malaria' (quoted in Connor, 2004, p. 1).

The *Compendium* does open up another avenue closely allied to issues of the 'common good' by its support in n. 468 for the 'right to a safe and healthy environment'. Pope John Paul II referred to this emerging juridical consensus in an address to the European Commission and Court of Human Rights in Strasbourg on 8 October 1988. The Pope was aware that the environmental justice movements and human rights movements are increasingly applying a rights-based strategy to confront global devastation. This particular right is seen within the wider expansion of the notion of human rights in the past two decades. These include the right to an adequate standard of living, the right to education, the right to food and water, the right to adequate provisions for remaining healthy and the right to housing and work.

The right to a healthy environment requires a healthy habitat. This precludes anything that might damage the life-sustaining processes of the planet, which includes access to clean water, fresh air and fertile soils free from toxins or hazards that would threaten human well-being. If, as we know, global warming is going to make the climatic conditions for the earth and humans extremely unpleasant, then campaigns to promote action on global warming could be fought under the banner of a right to a stable climate.

For some strange reason, eight articles in a chapter of a mere 15 pages in the *Compendium* are devoted to biotechnology. Article 473 approves of recombinant DNA technology when its states that the human person does not commit an illicit act when, out of respect for the order, beauty and usefulness of individual living beings and their function in the ecosystem, he intervenes by modifying some of their characteristics or properties. This cannot refer to traditional forms of breeding because these have been practised for 10,000 years, since the beginning of agriculture. It must refer to recombinant DNA technology. The sentence must have been smuggled into the text without the knowledge of the President of the Pontifical Council for Justice and Peace, Cardinal Renato Martino, since he continues to insist that the Vatican has not made up its mind on plant and animal biotechnology. Jesus Verala, Bishop Emiritus of Sorsogen in the Philippines, has used this text in conferences organised by the biotech industry to justify his support for genetic engineering.

Intergenerational Justice

Another source for shaping a theology and morality to underpin action on climate change and other ecological issues comes from a concern for intergenerational justice. Traditional ethical concerns normally dealt with the impact of our behaviour on individuals or communities in the here-and-now or the immediate future. This is no longer an adequate framework because this generation, through its powerful technologies, is bringing about massive changes to the fabric of the earth, which will affect in a negative way every succeeding generation of humans and other creatures. The basic principle that arises from this ethical concern is that future generations have the right to inherit a world as fertile and as beautiful as the one that we inhabit. This new moral context is recognised in n. 470 of the *Compendium of the Social Doctrine of the Church*. It states:

> From a moral perspective based on equity and intergenerational solidarity, it will be necessary to continue, through the contribution of the scientific community, to identify new sources of energy, develop alternative sources and increase the security level of nuclear energy.

Concern for future generations would also help us counteract the following attitude that is prevalent today among many people, especially politicians and bureaucrats. If something is not going to happen on my watch, then I'll leave it to my successor to deal with it, even though I know what I am doing now will exacerbate the problem and maybe create a situation that might be irreversible.

In response to this attitude, the church needs to develop its teaching on sustainability and on the 'precautionary principle'. We need to reformulate the idea of sustainable development that was the bedrock of the Brundtland Report published as *Our Common Future* in 1987. It defined sustainable development as seeking 'to meet the needs and aspirations of the present without compromising the ability to meet those of the future'. Then it went on to affirm that

> far from requiring the cessation of economic growth, it recognises that the problems of poverty and underdevelopment cannot be solved unless we have a new era of growth in which developing countries play a large role and reap large benefits. (p. 40)

Almost 20 years later, any ecological evaluation of the impact of economic growth in either the Celtic Tiger economy of Ireland or the two-digit GDP annual growth of the Chinese economy should make it absolutely clear that the Western, oil-dependent kinds of growth that China and India are now pursuing are environmentally unsustainable as well as devastating. We need to be reminded that the earth is finite and that we must live in a way that is fair and just towards future generations of humans and other creatures.

The precautionary principle is another moral principle that is mentioned in Number 469 of *The Compendium of the Social Teachings of the Church*. This document presents the 'precautionary principle' in the context of making practical decisions about the impact of an action on human health or environmental well-being when contradictory scientific opinions are being offered. The text states that in such a situation 'it may be appropriate to base evaluations on the precautionary principle, which does not mean applying rules but certain guidelines aimed at managing a situation of uncertainty.' The text implies that it is useful in dealing with difficult ethical situations.

However, the presentation of the precautionary principle is not so much a set of rules but *certain guidelines* that leave open the possibility for widening its scope to judge and challenge any kind of policies, especially economic ones, which may bring short-term economic benefits to a few at the cost of permanent ecological damage to an ecosystem or habitat. The *Compendium* does acknowledge this in n. 470 when it states that programmes of economic development must carefully consider 'the need to respect the integrity and cycles of nature because natural resources are limited and some are not renewable'. Once again, there is an assumption that this principle applies to a local situation. Now it must be applied in a situation where human activity is adversely changing climatic conditions for this and future generations.

We also need to understand the nature of irreversible ecological damage and its implications for future generations. The potential damage from global warming to the earth and the peoples of the earth is enormous. Unless this generation stabilises the emissions of global warming gases, then the consequences are inevitable and irreversible in geological time. It is an extraordinary and awesome moment in human and earth affairs that the behaviour of one or two generations can have such profound and irreversible impact, not just on human history, but on the planet as well.

Preferential Option for the Poor

Another principle that is helpful in the search for an ecological theology is the preferential option for the poor. This is a relatively recent moral principle that emerged, especially in Latin America, during the second part of the 20th century. It is now enshrined in Catholic social teaching. It challenges individuals and societies to examine ethical and economic choices from the point of view of how it will affect poor people, not just in their locality, but globally as well (*Compendium of the Social Doctrine of the Church*, n. 59). Will these ethical and economic choices enhance the life of the poor or further impoverish them?

One of the abiding tragedies and ironies in reflecting on global warming is that the poor, who have contributed least to it, will suffer most. The World Council of Churches' document on climate change, *Sign of Peril, Test of Faith*, includes a chart on page 11 that attempts to calculate emissions of CO_2 from various countries between 1800 and 1988. We find that according to the chart North America contributed 32.2 per cent, Europe's contribution was 26.1 per cent, Latin America was 3.8 per cent and China was 5.5 per cent. China's carbon dioxide emission has grown enormously since. It is now estimated that by 2025 China will have overtaken the US as the top emitter of greenhouse gases if the present trend of fossil fuel use continues (McCarthy,

2005, p. 1). Archbishop Desmond Tutu put the problem of global warming very succinctly in his foreword to the recent publication *Africa: Up in Smoke?*

> The world's wealthiest countries have emitted more than their fair share of greenhouse gases. Resultant floods, droughts and other climate change impacts continue to fall disproportionately on the world's poorest people and countries, many of which are in Africa. (in Simms, 2005, p. 1)

The church community and all humankind need to respond to the plight of the poor. Solidarity was a concept much beloved of Pope John Paul II. In his Encyclical *Sollicitudo Rei Socialis* (Concern for Social Realities 1987, n. 38) he describes solidarity

> not as a feeling of vague compassion or shallow distress at the misfortunes of so many people, both near and far. On the contrary, it is a firm and persevering determination to commit oneself to the common good: that is to say the good of all and of each individual, because we are all really responsible for all. (par. 37)

In the context of the deepening ecological crisis, solidarity acknowledges that we are increasingly bound together as members of the earth community. In her overview of the statement on ecology from the Holy See, Sister Marjorie Keenan (2002, p. 38) writes that the 'concept of solidarity also extends to nature'. We are responsible for the well-being of the poor and all creation. Both these destinies are intertwined. We will either bequeath to the next generation of all life a fruitful, beautiful, and vibrant planet for the well-being of all creatures, or one in which all future generations will be diminished. In such a barren and polluted world future generations will be forced to live amid the ruins, not merely of the technological world, but of the natural world itself.

Concern for the Wider Earth Community

Another element in the moral framework is a concern for the wider earth community. The wider earth community encompasses all life. This perspective on life has only begun to emerge in recent times. Unfortunately, it is not completely central to the teachings of Vatican Congregations or Councils. Today moral theologians are arguing that other creatures have more than just instrumental value for humans as sources of food, clothing and medicine. The wider earth community is not recognised as having intrinsic value in itself. Anyone who studies nature knows that God has taken as much care in creating other species, especially the smaller creatures, as he has in creating the human. After all, humans only emerged over two million years ago, which is merely the flick of an eyelid in the 3.7 billion years of life on earth. God loves other creatures and we humans are linked to them through close biological and genetic bonding. Given our present ecological challenges, either the whole biosphere will prosper or we will all go down together.

Preaching the Gospel of Life

The churches' response to the destruction of entire ecosystems and the extinction of an enormous number of creatures should be to preach and embody a gospel of life. It will involve challenging some of the most powerful business groups in the world today. In Britain, business representatives have criticised their government's modest targets to reduce carbon dioxide emissions on the basis that this would risk sacrificing British jobs. Some in the business community appear to put short-term profits before the long-term well-being of the planet. Religious leaders are remiss in their prophetic ministry if they are unwilling to challenge such ultimately destructive policies.

In the context of preaching a gospel of life, it is important to revisit the question of human population levels on this planet. *Populorum Progressio* admits that

> there is no denying that the accelerated rate of population growth brings many added difficulties to the problems of development where the size of the population grows more rapidly than the quantity of available resources to such a degree that things seem to have reached an impasse ... it is for parents to take a thorough look at the matter and decide on the number of their children. This is an obligation they take on themselves, before their children already born, and before the community to which they belong – following the dictates of their own consciences informed by God's law authentically interpreted, and bolstered by their trust in him. (n. 37)

When the encyclical appeared, some commentators felt that it might signal a change in the Catholic Church's position on artificial methods of birth control. This did not happen. I have explored the population issue in greater detail in my book, *The*

Greening of the Church, where I made the point that the earth's carrying capacity for different levels of population was not addressed in the 1968 encyclical *Humanae Vitae.* Today there is an urgent need to revisit the population issue. It is important to state that a fall in population levels will not, of itself, reduce the stress on the planet unless it is accompanied by a drop in our consumption patterns. Nevertheless, the time is now ripe for the Catholic Church to revisit its teaching on birth control.

It would be ironic if a strict adherence to *Humanae Vitae,* which sets out to promote respect for life, undermined, in the longer term, the conditions that are necessary for human life in the future. An ecological ethical perspective must focus on reality in a holistic way, rather than on the interaction of individual entities or actors. We are living at the time of a mega-extinction spasm. This will get much worse unless humans show a greater willingness to share the global commons with other species.

Time to change – Now

It is important that the changes begin now. We are certainly living in a time of unprecedented crisis for the natural world. From a Christian theological perspective we are living in a *kairos* moment. It demands concrete choices for individuals and institutions to help bring about this new age. We need inspired political leadership because, no matter what individuals do to address global warming, if the political and economic community does not come on board little will be achieved. We need politicians such as Al Gore, former vice-president of the US, who have the courage to explain to the public what is at stake in the whole area of global warming and who will lead people to make the kind of changes that will be necessary. Carbon taxes are merely the beginning of a comprehensive approach that lessens our use of fossil fuel and develops a range of alternative energy sources.

The church as a 'sign raised up among the nations' should be in the forefront of these efforts. Those in positions of authority in the churches must also give effective leadership. The editorial in *The Tablet* newspaper for 4 November 2006 calls on the papacy to give leadership in tackling global environmental destruction.

The editor writes that

> it is time for the Catholic Church to renew its theology of creation, a task worthy of a papal encyclical and indeed a pope like Benedict. Science and economics cannot save the planet without the will to do so. Religion, and possibly only religion, can provide that will.

On a religious level, we should try to evolve a theology, spirituality and missiology that are sensitive to the presence of God in the natural world. Rituals that celebrate God's presence are vitally important in order to reconnect us in an integral way with the natural world. We must develop these for our homes, schools, and Christian communities. This will call forth creativities that at present lie dormant in the community of the church.

References

Compendium of the Social Doctrine of the Church (2004) Dublin: Veritas Publications.

Connor, Steve (2004) 'US climate policy is a bigger threat to world than terrorism', *The Independent*, 9 January 2004, p. 1.

Keenan, Marjorie, RSHM (2000) *Care For Creation: Human Activity and the Environment*, Vatican City: Libreria Editrice Vaticana.

Keenan, Marjorie, RSHM (2002) *From Stockholm to Johannesburg: an historical overview of the concern of the Holy See for the environment*, Vatican City: Pontifical Council for Justice and Peace.

McCarthy Michael (2005) 'The China Crisis', *The Independent*, 19 October 2005, p. 1.

McDonagh, Seán (1990) *The Greening of the Church*, London: Chapman.

Our Common Future: The World Commission on Environment and Development, (1987) Oxford: Oxford University Press.

Pearce, Fred (2006) 'Global meltdown', *The Guardian*, 30 August 2006, p 8.

Taylor, Andrew (2004) 'Jobs warning over tough move on emissions', *Financial Times*, 20 January 2004.

Simms, Andrew (2005) *Africa: up in smoke? The second report from the Working Group on Climate Change and Development*, London: New Economics Foundation, International Institute for Environment and Development.

World Council of Churches (1994) *Sign of Peril, Test of Faith, Accelerated Climate Change*, Geneva: World Council of Churches

World Council of Churches (2002) *Solidarity with the Victims of Climate Change, Reflections on the World Council of Churches' Response to Climate Change*, Geneva: World Council of Churches.

Lessons Learned: Populorum Progressio
Forty Years on

Pete Henriot SJ

'Is it possible – indeed, is it desirable – to get very excited about a papal document written some four decades ago?' That is the question I used to begin a presentation in January 2006 at a forum convened by CIDSE entitled 'The Church Speaking Out on Social Justice Today.' I answered the question with a modest yes, citing the many good points raised in Paul VI's *Populorum Progressio*, while also noting some shortcomings and absences.

Were I to answer that question today, after reading the several essays presented in this book produced by the International Jesuit Network for Development (IJND), my answer would not be such a modest yes. Rather it would be a resounding yes, yes, yes! Indeed, reflections on the essays, joined with a rereading of this encyclical, give me many reasons for getting very excited. True, this encyclical was written at a time different in so many ways from today – a pre-internet world and a pre 9/11 world, a world belligerently divided into communist and capitalist camps, a world only beginning to be challenged by the women's movement and ecological concerns, and a world untouched by the 25-year influence of John Paul II, the Catholic Church's most influential leader in the 20th century.

But the lessons that can be learned from *Populorum Progressio* are so very relevant to our contemporary scene that I do get enthused about it and I am pleased to share a bit of that enthusiasm in this concluding chapter of our IJND book. I write from a perspective of living for almost two decades in Zambia, one of the richest countries in Africa in terms of natural and human resources, but one of the poorest countries in the world in terms of living standards measured by the United Nations *Human Development Index*. (We are 165 out of 177 on the 2006 UNDP Index.) And I write from an apostolate of devoting energies to development research, education and advocacy in an effort to address that shocking dichotomy between riches and poverty.

Without simply repeating the excellent points raised by the wide spectrum of authors on a varied set of topics, let me summarise the lessons under three headings and then point to some action responses that seem very pertinent to a meaningful celebration. Yes, I believe we need more action than applause in celebrating *Populorum Progressio* at this time. The power of this encyclical and its relevance today seem to me to lie in three lessons that can be drawn from reading the text and reflecting on the essays in this book.

- First, good social analysis presents a picture of development that is intellectually convincing and politically compelling.
- Second, good moral foundations lay the groundwork for interventions that are relevant to public policy debates and decisions.
- Third, good social mobilisation moves the discussion out of the realm of theory into the real world of politics.

You can see that the three lessons I choose to emphasise from the document all have political dimensions. That is not simply because I write as a political scientist but also because I am committed to political action to change a world that is, in the words of *Populorum Progressio*, 'sick' (n. 66) and in the words of the author of another chapter in this collection, Sobrino, 'dehumanised'.

Good Social Analysis

Paul VI's view of the world is 'optimistic' in the sense of seeing a world on the course of coming closer to the Creator and the Creator's good plans. Thus he can write: 'Humanity is advancing along the path of history like the waves of a rising tide encroaching gradually on the shore' (n. 17). He sees the international cooperation of groups like the United Nations as a response to the vocation 'to bring not some people but all peoples to treat each other as sisters and brothers' (n. 78). For those who would view such optimism, such fresh hope, as unrealistic and purely utopian, he makes a direct challenge: 'It may be that these persons are not realistic enough, and that they have not perceived the dynamism of a world which desires to live more fraternally – a world which, in spite of its ignorance, its mistakes and even its sins, its relapse into a barbarism and its wanderings far from the road of salvation, is, even unawares, taking slow but sure steps towards its Creator' (n. 79).

But Paul's view of the world is also 'pessimistic' in that he sees so many problems that block the authentic development for which our shared humanity longs. He can call the world of his time 'sick' because it ignores the tremendous gaps between rich and poor and continues wasteful spending on national and personal ostentation and on the arms race. The repeated statistical pictures painted by several of the authors in this book simply make evident the mistakes, sins, barbarism and wanderings the Pope noted in his day – and which are so much more compounded in today's world of wars, terrorism, genocide, gender abuse, starvation and ecological destruction.

So how can we balance the 'optimistic' tone with the 'pessimistic' view in learning from *Populorum Progressio*? I believe the response lies in noting the keen social analysis of Paul, by no means complete but still quite challenging. Several of the authors in this book – for example, Cejka on peace, Torres on debt, Prakash on power, Kirby on globalisation, Zulu on trade – highlight that the encyclical does indeed rely on structural analysis to make its points.

Often cited is the discussion by Paul of international trade – a discussion that rings well with today's analysis of the World Trade Organisation (WTO). In paragraphs 56 to 61, Paul dwells on the inherited patters of injustice in trading relationships, the unreality of 'free trade' regimes among nations of excessive inequalities of economic power, the unfairness of agricultural subsidies of rich countries, the need to go beyond mere market considerations if poor countries are to move forward. This is certainly contemporary social analysis, as Zulu notes in his discussion of the impact of 'free trade' that is not 'fair trade' and hence not 'just trade'.

But it is not only in discussing trade that the encyclical shows good social analysis. Its link between development and peace is rooted in an analysis of the conditions that give rise to peace. For peace is seen not simply as the absence of conflict but the presence of the necessities for peace, the structures and practices of justice (n. 76). Cejka summarises well the teachings related to peace that are found in *Populorum Progressio*. She notes that it teaches that to work against poverty by promoting economic, moral and spiritual development is to advance the cause of peace. As Paul notes, 'To wage war on misery and to struggle against injustice is to promote, along with improved conditions, the human and spiritual progress of all people, and therefore the common good of humanity' (n. 76). Muhigirwa applies that analysis in explaining the current challenge to peaceful life in Africa.

But having pointed to good social analysis that offers lessons today, I cannot pass over lightly the critique of where Paul's analysis fails to take into account two immense challenges of today – thereby rendering his message in need of strong correction. First, as Riley points out, *Populorum Progressio* is lacking in any sign of appreciation of the gender issues that are so central to any adequate development analysis and action. This might be understandable – the encyclical is the outcome of a perpetuated culture of male dominance. But it means that its perspective is narrow and faulty in understanding adequately the power dimensions of the project of authentic development.

The second obvious lack of analytical comprehensiveness is noted by McDonagh, the failure to offer an ecological critique. Indeed, the encyclical is silent on a central challenge of our time, the massive and often irreducible destruction of the environment. The author critiques what he terms a 'homocentric' focus in *Populorum Progressio* that is characteristic of Catholic social teaching (CST) – citing the strong emphasis of paragraph 22 on the human's right to find in the world whatever is necessary for human use. There is no acknowledgement of what should be our respect for the other members of the community of creation.

While acknowledging the significant lacunae in some of the analysis in the encyclical, I still can note its richness in a structural understanding of reality, manifested for instance, in Paul's early statement that 'Today the principal fact that we must all recognise is that the social question has become worldwide' (n. 3). To begin this way opens up to the analysis so necessary to understand and respond to globalisation, the context of development in our time.

Why is the social analysis so keen in this document? I would venture to say that one reason is that it is a specifically unique and laudable contribution of Paul VI to the CST tradition that in his encyclical he readily cites a wide range of economic and ethical writers on development. The list includes, for example, J.-L. Lebret, Colin Clark, O. v. Nell-Breuning, Jacques Maritain, M.-D. Chenu, and H. de Lubac. He opened himself up to good analysis from 'outside' the Vatican walls – something that unfortunately does not commonly characterise many CST documents.

Good Moral Foundation

It is to be expected that a major CST document would be a teacher of good morals and sound ethics. But I believe that today we can particularly learn from the fundamental moral teaching of *Populorum Progressio* about development: it must be human-centred. (This emphasis needs, as briefly cited in the ecological discussion above, to be broadened to include the human's place in the community of creation.)

As Kirby notes very strongly in his essay, it presents a definition of development that would become a foundation for one of the most influential development actors on the international scene today, the United Nations Development Programme (UNDP). Paul states clearly that authentic development is 'for each and all the transition from less human conditions to those which are more human' (n. 20). Since human conditions are what matters, the UNDP now provides in its influential *Human Development Index* (HDI) the standard measurement of what is really happening to people, in contrast to what is happening to the economy. For example, abstract economic measurements such as rate of investment are replaced by concrete human measurements of life expectancy.

What I am saying is that a moral foundation that primarily values the human person immediately has consequences in what we consider important for the development agenda. Kufekisa-Akapelwa highlights this in her discussion of the relationship between human rights and development. Kelly can base his development-oriented approach to meeting the challenge of the HIV/AIDS pandemic because he sees how contradictory and destructive the spread of HIV/AIDS is to the 'more human' conditions that *Populorum Progressio* defines as the outcome of authentic development. Indeed, Riley's disappointment with the lack of gender focus in the document can be seen, I believe, as recognition of Paul's short-sightedness in an emphasis that overly identifies the 'human' with the 'male'.

A second strong moral foundation of *Populorum Progressio* is certainly its discussion of solidarity. Indeed, Paul anticipates much of the discussion around the CST concept of solidarity that would follow in the writings of John Paul II. Paul writes: 'There is no progress toward the complete development of women and men without the simultaneous development of all humanity in the spirit of solidarity' (n. 43). What is this solidarity? I would see it as the moral force that moves us beyond the empirical reality of economic interdependence to the ethical reality of human interconnectedness. It is related, I believe, to the African understanding of *ubuntu*: 'I am because we are and we are because I am.' My worth is always interrelated with the worth of the community to which I belong.

To describe the contrast between development and underdevelopment, Prakash highlights a set of opposing poles such as power and powerlessness, inclusion and exclusion, affluence and destitution, consumption and starvation. These are, in his view, structural relationships and not simply factual conditions. Herein lies the influence of the moral foundation of solidarity. For it is simply not possible to live humanly in a world where so many of our sisters and brothers struggle to survive. Sobrino makes this point again and again in describing the 'inhumanness' of our global situation today. Paul makes the point in stating that avarice – the exclusive pursuit of possessions – is for nations and individual persons 'the most evident form of moral underdevelopment' (n. 19).

Much more could be said about the moral emphasis on what makes up true development. But it should be evident that *Populorum Progressio*'s good moral foundation is a strong reason for its lasting value today. And it is a major contribution to the political discourse that characterises, for example, the current debate over the Millennium Development Goals (MDGs), both their worth and the process necessary to achieve them.

Good Popular Mobilisation

Surely one of the lasting strengths of *Populorum Progressio* is its emphasis on action, indeed, on urgent action. Paul makes an appeal to mobilise a response to the situation at hand, for 'Changes are necessary, basic reforms are indispensable' (n. 81). He issues a clarion call:

> We want to be clearly understood: the present situation must be faced with courage and the injustices linked with it must be fought against and overcome. Development demands bold transformations, innovations that go deep. Urgent reforms should be undertaken without delay (n. 32).

Again, in condemning wasteful expenditures, for example, through spending on national or personal ostentation or on the arms race, Paul voices his urgency with the plea 'Would that those in authority listened to our plea before it is too late' (n. 53).

Regarding the steps to be taken to meet that urgency he expresses, Paul makes an appeal to a cross-section of society to be mobilised for action. Christians and non-Christians, delegates to international organisations, government officials, women and men in the press, educators: 'all of you, each in your own way, are the builders of a new world' (n. 83).

Given the distance of 40 years, we can and should do some evaluation about whether Paul's message of urgency and appeal for action was really heard and effectively responded to. But it is encouraging in reading the essays in this book to note where effective social mobilisation for action has in effect occurred and brought about change. Zulu highlights the successes of the Jubilee movement to cancel debt, Muhigirwa points to the potential of NEPAD to make an impact on development in Africa, Torres notes the growing influence of numerous social movements and networks within civil society that work to transform the economies that exclude the majority of the world's population from a just distribution of goods.

The mobilising impact of *Populorum Progressio* is recognised by

Kilcullen as a major influence in the establishment of Trócaire, the Catholic development agency in Ireland. Other similar agencies can also trace their foundation to the strong appeals in this document. And surely one of the very significant forces for mobilising social action in the past several decades has been the establishment throughout the world of Justice and Peace Commissions, the offspring of the Pontifical Commission so strongly endorsed in the encyclical (n. 5).

Both Cejka and Riley point to hindrances to the effective social mobilisation necessary to implement the vision and values of Paul's picture of development. Internal church anomalies in the treatment of women, over-focus on personal morality issues, debilitating scandals within the ranks of clergy and hierarchy – these are just a few of the unfortunate factors that slow down the social mobilisation called for by Paul. They need to be addressed honestly and effectively today if we are going to move forward in implementing his vision.

Concluding Lessons
In conclusion, let me suggest two additional lessons that can be drawn from *Populorum Progressio* and the essays in this book that reflect on its message. These are rather obvious lessons, but their importance bears repeating.

First, the call to justice must never be muted in our church's response to the complex problems of the day. That is, we must never let the challenging dimensions of these problems distract us into merely palliative responses that do not really go to the root causes of unjust systems and situations. Structural change is necessary in dealing with the issues described and analysed in this book, for example debt, trade, governance, gender, environment, HIV / AIDS, peace, migration, and globalisation.

In other words, charity is no substitute for justice. I believe that Paul acknowledges that quite clearly. For public and private funds, gifts and loans, no matter how generous, are not sufficient to eliminate hunger or reduce poverty, if not linked to the effort for 'building a world where all people, no matter what their race, religion or nationality, can live fully human lives, freed from servitude imposed on them by others or by natural forces over which they have not sufficient control; a world where freedom is not an empty word...' (n. 47).

Benedict XVI's first encyclical letter, *Deus Caritas Est* (God Is Love), while emphasising so very strongly the importance of love, does not depart from the central teaching that the invitation to charity is never far from the call to justice. Such, of course, is a central message in the great document of the 1971 Synod of Bishops, *Justice in the World*:

> Christian love of neighbour and justice cannot be separated. For love implies an absolute demand for justice, namely a recognition of the dignity and rights of one's neighbour. Justice attains its inner fullness only in love (n. 34).

Second, the need to communicate more widely and effectively the message of the church's social teaching has never been more urgent. The work of the church and civil society in confronting the tragic injustices of our day should be grounded in the CST to provide clarity, inspiration, motivation and sustainability. Several years ago, I collaborated with some colleagues in producing a book with the catchy title, *Catholic Social Teaching: Our Best Kept Secret*. The book has gone through several editions and remains quite popular. And unfortunately, its title is still all too true! Too many seminaries do not educate students about the CST, too many religious leaders do not inform their congregations about its importance, too many political and business officials do not know of its relevance.

In the work of a recently established research and education project based in Harare, Zimbabwe, the African Forum for Catholic Social Teaching (AFCAST), we say that there is a value-added dimension in the debates and decisions of public policy that is offered by the social teaching. This CST that we deal with is not abstract but concrete, not neutral but committed, not polite but prophetic. It does not cite authors but applies principles. In the African context, this means dealing with issues of justice, development, peace and the integrity of creation. Value dimensions of these issues should not be 'our best kept secret.'

Surely one of the happy consequences of recalling the significance of *Populorum Progressio* should be a heightened awareness of, and deepened appreciation for, the riches of our CST. And this should encourage us to spread the CST message more widely so that it might change the world we live in today and that we leave for our children tomorrow. The many and varied authors of essays in this book surely believe that. And it is our hope and prayer that the readers of the book will share that same belief.

Populorum Progressio

Paraphrased Outline of the Encyclical

Jim Hug SJ

Addressed to Catholics and all people of good will

26 March 1967

1.   The first sentence identifies the people as the subject of their own development, 'making very great efforts to free themselves from the hardship of hunger, poverty ... and demanding that greater value be in fact set upon their qualities as human beings'. The church supports them and urges people to recognise that the cooperation of all is urgently needed.

2.   *Populorum Progressio* (PP) builds on the social teaching tradition from Popes Leo XIII to John XXIII.

3.   The social question now extends to all human relations. The hungry are calling for help and the church calls each individual motivated by love to listen to their brothers and sisters.

4.   Pope Paul experienced the struggle in his own travels to South America, Africa, Palestine and India. He notes the rich personal and cultural resources they have that are 'entangled and, so to say, hemmed in' by poverty.

5.   The Pope establishes the Commission for Justice and Peace to make all the people of God aware of the struggles, to promote development, foster social justice, and seek assistance for the poorer nations to provide their own development.

6.   Pope Paul again paints the picture of the people themselves longing and working for social and economic progress while 'living in conditions which frustrate their just desires', seeking development after achieving political independence.

7.   Pope Paul addresses the legacy of colonialism, acknowledging how some colonising countries left their colonies with badly structured economies reliant on a single com-

modity, but also noting that others transferred skills and institutions that are good, but not sufficient for today.

8. The structures left behind are not suited to cope with a modern economy. Without regulation of modern technological civilisation, inequalities among peoples will grow worse.

9. There are vast inequalities in goods, but even more in the exercise of power.

10. The conflict between traditional civilisations and industrial civilisation lead to generational conflicts. Often ancestral institutions and traditional moral, spiritual and religious values are perverted or lost.

11. This critical situation tempts to populism, rebellion and totalitarianism.

12. Pope Paul offers a tribute to the positive role of missionaries, at the same time acknowledging the existence of cultural imperialism among missionaries.

13. Church and state are independent authorities, each supreme in its own sphere. The church shares human aspirations and is pained when they are so often frustrated – so it offers its understanding of 'human affairs in their totality'.

14. Genuine development integrates the economic into the totality of human life for all people.

15. Each is to promote his/her own progress. Each is the 'chief architect' of his/her own development of the seeds of aptitudes and qualities planted at birth – even though influenced by others and the environment.

16. Developing our gifts is our responsibility and who we become is drawn up into Christ.

17. As social beings, each is called to work for the full development of the whole human society. As we benefit from earlier generations, we have responsibilities for those who come after us.

18. Working to provide necessities is a duty of each person.

But seeking ever more goods and power can drive people to materialism and stifles their souls.

19. It is important to work to develop as a person, but having too many possessions imprisons us, sets us in competition and is divisive in communities. People 'infected with the vice of avarice give clearest evidence of moral under-development'.

20. More than technical knowledge, we need wisdom to promote a humanism or spirituality by which we accept love, friendship, prayer and contemplation as far greater blessings than possessions. True development consists in 'each and everyone's passing from less human to more human living conditions'.

21. Pope Paul defines less-human and more-human living conditions:

    a. Less-human:
       i. Destitution, lack of minimum subsistence necessary
      ii. Those almost crushed by moral deficiency brought on themselves by excessive self-love
     iii. Those oppressed by social structures created by abuses of ownership or power, exploitation of workers or unjust transactions

    b. More-human:
      iv. Possession of necessities, winning the struggle against social ills, broader knowledge, acquisition of culture
      v. Increased esteem for the dignity of others
     vi. An inclination for the spirit of poverty
    vii. Cooperation for the common good, the will for peace
   viii. Recognition of God as source and end of these blessings
    ix. Faith

22. Creation is for all humanity, to provide for the necessities of each and all. Vatican II states: 'God destined the earth with all that it contains for the use of all people and all

nations, in such a way that created things in fair share should accrue to all ... under the leadership of justice with charity as a companion. All other rights ... including property rights and the right of free trade must be subordinated to this norm; they must ... expedite its application.'

23. Anyone who observes the needs of others and doesn't respond does not have God's love. The patristic writers called it theft to have more than needed when others don't have enough. Private ownership is not an unconditional right; it must be used for the common good. If conflicts arise, public authorities need to seek a solution in dialogue.

24. The common good can require expropriation of property. Excessive profit for personal advantage should be prohibited, as should capital flight for private advantage.

25. Industrialisation can promote both economic growth and human progress.

26. But through it 'unbridled liberalism' has entered and paved the way for the tyranny of the 'internationalism of finance or international imperialism'. Pope Paul defines 'unbridled liberalism' as: 'profit was considered the chief incentive to foster economic development, competition the supreme law of economics, private ownership of the means of production an absolute right which recognises neither limits nor concomitant social duty.'

27. Reflections on work as a means of personal development, cooperation with God in creation, growing in community.

28. Work by promising money, pleasure and power can incite excessive self-love or discord; or it can cause personal development and love of neighbour. It must not enslave the worker. It must be based on intelligence and freedom; it should be a partnership of human beings that serves human dignity.

29. The gap between rich and poor is widening: we must make haste, but with care for good agrarian reform and industrialisation.

30. When entire populations lack necessities and are totally dominated, the situation cries out to God for punishment – and tempts violent response.

31. In most cases insurrection brings on new injustices. We can't fight existing evil in such a way that we bring on greater misfortune.

32. We must struggle against these injustices courageously, boldly and urgently, especially those with the most influence. Let them give of their possessions as an example.

33. Individual initiative and market competition will not assure successful development; they will result in greater disparities and injustice. Public authorities need to institute social programmes to make up for the deficiencies of the activities of individuals and markets to serve the common good. They should engage individuals and intermediary organisations in doing this.

34. Programmes to increase production must serve the whole human person. They should lessen inequalities, remove discrimination, free people from the bonds of servitude, and enable them to improve their condition in the temporal order, achieve moral development and perfect 'their spiritual endowments'. Producing wealth is not enough: it must be distributed. The dangers of technocracy need to be recognised and avoided. All must serve human freedom, judgement, and authentic human progress.

35. Education and literacy are the essential bases for social progress and economic growth. They build self-esteem and inspire progress.

36. The person is fully human only within the framework of society and there the family plays the basic and most important role. The family's influence may have been excessive at times, but time honoured social frameworks are still necessary.

37. Population pressures can frustrate efforts at development. Public authorities can provide information on this but not violate the rights of matrimony and procreation

essential to human dignity. It is the right of parents to decide how many children to have, following their properly instructed conscience.

38. Professional organisations beyond the family are important for educating people in the obligations of the common good.

39. Those organisations that are based on materialism and atheism must be rejected; but beyond that a pluralism of professional organisations and unions is good for safeguarding freedom and stimulating competition.

40. Cultural organisations are also essential for producing 'wise' people. The Second Vatican Council notes, 'many nations poorer in economic goods but richer in wisdom can confer on the rest a very great benefit.' It is critical to preserve traditional institutions that have true human values.

41. Poorer nations will be tempted by the development processes and cultural values of rich nations. They should discern which of these free the human spirit and which entangle it and lower the ideal of human life.

42. The complete form of humanism is 'to provide fully for the development of the whole person and of all persons'. It will be self-transcending, open to and reaching out to God as the absolute.

II

43. We must develop relationships and institutions to foster friendship between nations.

44. Serious obligations of the more affluent: 1) mutual relationship: aid; 2) social justice: improving trade relations; 3) charity: promoting a more human relationship for all in which all give and receive and the progress of some does not impede the development of others.

45. Today no one can be ignorant of countless hungry and suffering people.

46.   The church is responding and widening the circle of those cherished as neighbours.

47.   But this isn't enough. It is not simply about ending hunger or destitution. 'The point at issue is the establishment of a human society in which everyone, regardless of race, religion or nationality, can live a truly human life free from bondage imposed by people and the forces of nature not sufficiently mastered, a society in which freedom is not an empty word, and where Lazarus the poor person can sit at the same table as the rich person.' Are we ready to give of our own money? Pay more taxes to enable public authorities to respond? Pay higher prices for fair trade goods? Leave home to help other nations?

48.   The duty of solidarity among individuals holds for nations too. No nation should set aside its wealth just for itself, but should meet the needs of all its citizens for a dignified life and 'give assistance to the common development of the human race'.

49.   What is superfluous in nations must serve the needs of regions in want. Helping those 'closest to us' now applies to all in need throughout the world. The first to benefit will be the rich: if their avarice is not overcome, God's punishment and the anger of the poor will come down on them.

50.   Careful and concerted planning is essential; the responses must not be left to individual good will. Competition between development agencies must be avoided.

51.   Proposal of a World Fund for destitute peoples composed of parts of global military spending. Harmonious international cooperation is essential – instead of senseless rivalries – and can serve as the beginning of peaceful dialogue between nations.

52.   Bilateral and multilateral agreements, when joined with a general plan of mutual international assistance, can be very good. However, aid and technical assistance can still be used in the service of new forms of neo-colonialism.

53.   All expenditures of individuals and nations that squander

resources or fuel arms races while so many are hungry and destitute are 'a scandalous and intolerable crime'.

54. Dialogue is essential between aid providers and beneficiaries to achieve equitable distribution and meet the real needs of the people. This would avoid a debt crisis. Parasites are to be discouraged, but national sovereignty must be honoured. Collaboration 'without constraint and with equal dignity' and work to develop a civil society are essential.

55. People preoccupied with survival can't enter that kind of a relationship. We must see it as urgent to help in their development for the sake of their own life and of peace.

56. All efforts to help developing nations will be useless if the relief they provide is 'nullified as a result of variable trade relations' in which rich nations take back what they had given.

57. Poorer countries are dependent on wildly fluctuating commodities markets; richer nations grow richer relying on industrial products. Poorer nations grow poorer.

58. So 'free trade' cannot be the sole norm regulating international relations. It is advantageous only when the parties are fairly equal in resources.

59. Leo XIII stated that agreements made between parties that are too unequal may not be just. The law of free competition in trade too often creates economic dictatorship. Free trade is only fair 'when it is in accord with the demands of social justice'.

60. Developed countries act to make sure their economies remain balanced and work to make trade systems favourable to their own industries.

61. There must be equal standards between rich and poor nations; competition must be kept within limits that make it just and fair. International agreements on a sufficiently broad basis can be very helpful.

62. Other obstacles: nationalism and racism. Nationalism is understandable for newly independent nations and cultures, but it can be divisive and must be integrated with a universal vision.

63. Racism still is an obstacle to collaboration and is divisive.

64. There is hope in the potential for economic cooperation between developing countries and for regional development, with support from international organisations.

65. As world unity becomes greater, all peoples must be 'architects of their own fortune'. International relations must move away from being based on force to being based on friendship characterised by assistance, with mutual respect and collaboration to promote the improvement of all. Poorer nations have a just claim to play a greater role in the construction of a more fitting world that respects everyone's rights and duties.

66. The serious illness of society: severed bonds of community between people and nations.

67. So we must generously welcome others – especially the young, providing homes and hostels to protect them from loneliness, despair, and violent movements, and giving examples of charity and the highest spiritual values.

68. Many young people who go to study in affluent nations gain useful knowledge but lose esteem for the spiritual values of their home culture.

69. Emigrant workers must be welcomed; too often they live in inhuman conditions in order to send back money to their families.

70. We appeal to foreign investors/business people who show social sensitivity in their own countries but turn to harsh methods of serving only their own interests in poor countries. They should be leaders in social development and human progress there, training workers and managers and modelling employer/employee justice.

71. The increasing number of experts going abroad to help is good – they must go to help, not dominate, and show their work is filled with charity.

72. Technical skills must be integrated with genuine love and a readiness to share the skills with everyone and adapt to the new culture with respect. Workers should study the

history, special characteristics and knowledge of the country where they are guests. Goal: 'a contact of one culture with the other by which both will be enriched.'

73. A genuine dialogue between cultures will thrive where instilled with love and the desire to establish a civilisation of world solidarity. It will be advantageous when it achieves economic progress and greater spiritual and full human growth. This creates human bonds that promote peace.

74. Very many young people have become missionaries or chosen to work with organisations helping developing nations. Would that all Christians would respond to the call of the poor.

75. Let us pray for the human race to abolish poverty and misery – and match our prayer with firm determination to combat underdevelopment to the extent of our resources. Those animated with genuine love who work to discover the causes of misery and fight them are peacemakers.

76. Excessive social, economic and cultural inequalities among nations stir strife and imperil peace. Our charity must become more effective and generous. 'When we combat misery, and struggle against injustice we are providing not only for people's prosperity but also for their spiritual and moral development and are therefore promoting the welfare of the whole human race.' Peace requires constant work, attention to God's order, and a more perfect form of justice among people.

77. Nations can't develop alone. Agreements among poor nations regionally promote progress and lead to peace.

78. International cooperation demands institutions. We need to work toward establishing a world authority 'capable of acting effectively in the juridical and political sphere'.

79. The 'dynamics of this age' show a desire to live in greater harmony and a more human way of life. We are taking 'slow but sure steps' towards a greater humanity and moving in this direction will require effort and sacrifice.

80. It is urgent to act now. At stake: survival of children, the

possibility for families to live humanly, and the peace of the world and the survival of civilisation.

81. *Populorum Progressio* is addressed to the church: to the laity working to improve the temporal order by their planning and initiative and permeate it with the spirit of the gospel and a Christian sense of life; to the hierarchy to teach and explain the moral laws and precepts involved; to Catholics in wealthy countries to lead in efforts to see that 'in all nations just and equitable laws be founded on moral principles'.

82. And to all Christians: help people to restrain egoism, arrogance and cooperate to open a way for all to a more human life. And to non-Christian religious communities to work for conditions worthy of children of God.

83. And to all of good will: people of all walks of life, such as delegates to international organisations, government officials, educators, journalists.

84. Heads of state: join your nations to all people and persuade them to give. Ambassadors to international organisations: pursue a policy of mutual international cooperation.

85. All of good will: seek and you will find: open ways through giving and receiving mutual aid, study in greater depth, and greater love is needed to create a more human way of life.

86. Genuine development: to be found in an economy adjusted to the welfare of the human person and in daily sustenance provided for all, the source, as it were, of love and a clear sign of the help of Divine Providence.

87. Today no one doubts that 'development is synonymous with peace'. We urge a prompt response to our appeal.

Given at Rome at St Peter's on the twenty-sixth day of March, the feast of the Resurrection of Our Lord Jesus Christ, 1967.

Contributors

MARY ANN CEJKA is Associate Researcher at the Center for Mission Research and Study at Maryknoll. She was co-director of a major three-year research study on how local communities in ten different parts of the world face the challenge of grassroots peacemaking. The results of this study were published in *Artisans of Peace: Grassroots Peacemaking among Christian Communities*, which was co-edited by Thomas Bamat (Orbis Books, 2003). The author of many articles on spirituality and peace, she is a longtime activist for peace and for Catholic Church reform. She holds a Master of Divinity degree from Yale and a PhD in psychology from Purdue University.

MIGUEL GONZALEZ MARTIN is the Coordinator of the Policy and Networking Department of ALBOAN, a Jesuit-sponsored development NGO in the Basque Country (Spain). He has served as a member of the Board of the International Jesuit Network for Development (IJND) since 2002, leading its work on governance-related issues. He holds degrees in Law (1995), Religious Sciences (2003) and Development Studies (2005). He currently is working on a PhD in development studies in the University of the Basque Country.

PETER J HENRIOT SJ is Director of the Jesuit Centre for Theological Reflection, Lusaka, Zambia. Before moving to Zambia in 1989, he was Director of the Center of Concern in Washington, DC. He specialises in the political economy of development in Africa and in the social teaching of the Catholic Church. He has published several books on social teaching and on development, including the widely used *Social Analysis: Linking Faith and Justice* (1980), which he wrote with Joe Holland. He holds a PhD in political science from the University of Chicago.

JAMES E HUG SJ is President of the Center of Concern, Washington, DC. He joined the Center in 1989 and his work focuses on research and education regarding issues of faith and economic justice. He has lectured, directed workshops and undertaken policy advocacy throughout the United States and in Europe, Africa, Asia and Australia. He is co-editor of *Catholic Social Teaching: Our Best Kept Secret* (revised fourth edition published by the Center of Concern and Orbis Books, 2003). He has contributed chapters to *Globalization and Catholic Social Thought: Present Crisis, Future Hope* (Novalis and Orbis Press, 2005) and *The Pastoral Circle Revisited: A Critical Quest for Truth and Transformation* (Orbis Books, 2005). He holds a PhD in Christian ethics from the University of Chicago.

JACK JONES ZULU is Economic Dimensions Programme Manager for the Southern African Regional Poverty Network (SARPN), based in

Johannesburg, South Africa. He was previously Coordinator of the Debt and Trade Project of the Jesuit Centre for Theological Reflection (JCTR) in Zambia. His work as a policy analyst with the Project led him to research the genesis and consequences of Zambia's external debt. Since JCTR hosts the Jubilee-Zambia campaign, he was also involved in advocacy for debt cancellation and for more effective use of the resources freed up in Zambia as a result of debt cancellation in 2005. He holds a Bachelor's degree in economics from the University of Zambia, and a Master's degree in economics from the University of Nairobi.

MICHAEL J KELLY SJ is currently an international consultant on HIV/ AIDS and education. He holds a doctorate in education from the University of Birmingham. He taught at the University of Zambia for many years, where he also served as Deputy Vice-Chancellor. Since retiring from his post in the University he has devoted his energies to exploring the causes, consequences and responses to the HIV/AIDS pandemic, with special focus on development, gender, children and social justice issues. Originally from Ireland, he moved to Zambia in the early 1950s and is a Zambian citizen.

JUSTIN KILCULLEN is Director of Trócaire, the Irish Catholic agency for overseas development. An architect by profession, he worked on social housing programmes both in the developing world and in Ireland before joining Trócaire in 1981 as project officer for Africa. He served as the agency's representative in Laos from 1988 to 1992. He is currently the President of Concord, a confederation of more than 1,500 European development NGOs across the European Union. In 2000, he was appointed as a Consultor to the Pontifical Council, *Cor Unum*, the Vatican body that coordinates the charitable work of the Catholic Church. He is a past President of CIDSE – an international alliance of fourteen Catholic development organisations in Europe and North America.

PEADAR KIRBY is Associate Professor at the School of Law and Government and Co-Director of the Centre for International Studies at Dublin City University, where he lectures on courses for the MA in International Relations and the MA in Globalisation. He was previously a journalist with *The Irish Times*, covering development and Latin American issues. He has published extensively on globalisation and development. His publications include: *Taming the Tiger: Social Exclusion in a Globalised Ireland* (co-edited with David Jacobson and Deiric Ó Broin, and published by Tasc with New Island Books, 2006); *Vulnerability and Violence: The Impact of Globalisation* (Pluto Press, 2006); *Introduction to Latin America: Twenty-First Century Challenges* (Sage, 2003); *The Celtic Tiger in Distress: Growth with Inequality in Ireland* (Palgrave, 2002). He holds a PhD from the London School of Economics.

MULIMA KUFEKISA-AKAPELWA is the Coordinator of the Governance Section of the Catholic Centre for Justice, Development and Peace (CCJDP) of the Catholic Bishops' Conference of Zambia. She holds a Bachelor's degree in social work from the University of Zambia and an MSc in comparative social research from Oxford University. Her work with the Catholic Justice and Peace Commission has included training programmes for parish Justice and Peace Committees throughout Zambia, and cooperation in national and regional economic analysis and advocacy work.

PRAKASH LOUIS SJ works in the Bihar Social Institute in the eastern part of India. He was previously Executive Director of the Indian Social Institute, New Delhi. He represented South Asia in the Society of Jesus Task Force on 'Globalisation and Marginalisation'. He contributes regularly to *Economic and Political Weekly* (journal of social sciences, published in Mumbai); *Mainstream, Social Change* and *Seminar*. His publications include: *People Power: The Naxalite Movement in Central Bihar* (2002) and *Political Sociology of Dalit Assertion* (2003). His doctoral studies, undertaken in the A.N. Sinha Institute of Social Studies, focused on the Radical Agrarian Movements in Central Bihar.

SEAN MCDONAGH SSC is a Columban missionary priest and lecturer who has campaigned and written extensively on the environment. His publications include: *Climate Change: The Challenge to All of Us* (2006), *The Death of Life: The Horror of Extinction* (2004), *Passion for the Earth* (1995), *Greening the Christian Millennium* (1999) and *Why are We Deaf to the Cry of the Earth?* (2001).

MUHIGIRWA RUSEMBUKA FERDINAND SJ is Provincial Coordinator of the Social Apostolate of the Society of Jesus in Central Africa; Director of CEPAS (*Centre d'Etudes pour l'Action Sociale*, Centre for Research and Social Action); Professor of Philosophy at the Jesuit Faculty Saint Pierre Canisius in Kimwenza, and Superior of the Saint Ignace Residence in Kinshasa. He obtained a ThM at the University of Toronto (1992), an STL at Regis College (Toronto, 1992), and a PhD in philosophy from the Gregorian University, Rome (1997), for which his thesis was 'Two Ways of Human Development According to Bernard Lonergan: Anticipation in Insight'.

EUGENE QUINN is National Director of the Jesuit Refugee Service (Ireland). He was previously Director of the Jesuit Centre for Faith and Justice in Dublin, and chaired the Debt Working Group of the International Jesuit Network for Development (IJND). He worked with the Jesuit Refugee Service (Bosnia) for two years as Director of the Mine Victims' Assistance Programme. He obtained an MA in international relations from Dublin City University in 2001. He is a qualified actuary and worked for ten years in the finance industry in Dublin.

MARIA RILEY OP is Coordinator of the Global Women's Project at the Center of Concern in Washington, DC. An Adrian Dominican Sister, she has been active in global women's issues since 1975 and attended the UN World Conferences on Women in Copenhagen, Nairobi and Beijing. She has been involved in founding several coalitions working to bring women's experience and women's perspective to macro-economic issues including Alt-WID (Alternative to Women in Development) and Women's Economic Alliance. She is the author of *Transforming Feminism* (1989); *Wisdom Seeks Her Way: Liberating the Power of Women's Spirituality* (1987); *In God's Image* (1987); *Women Faithful for the Future* (1987). She holds a PhD in English literature and in 1994 received a Doctorate in humane letters from Siena Heights University, Adrian, Michigan.

MARY ROBINSON was the first woman President of Ireland, serving from 1990 to 1997. She was United Nations High Commissioner for Human Rights from 1997 to 2002. She is currently leading a new project, 'Realizing Rights: The Ethical Globalisation Initiative', which is based in New York. Its goal is to bring the norms and standards of human rights into the globalisation process and to support capacity building in good governance in developing countries, with an initial focus on Africa. She is the recipient of numerous honours and awards throughout the world, and has been Honorary President of Oxfam International since 2002. She chairs the Council of Women World Leaders and is Vice-President of the Club of Madrid. She was educated at the University of Dublin (Trinity College), King's Inns Dublin and Harvard Law School.

JON SOBRINO SJ is professor of theology at the Universidad de America Central (UCA), El Salvador. He was a close collaborator with Óscar Romero, Archbishop of El Salvador, who was assassinated in 1980. Fr Sobrino lived in the community of Jesuits who, along with their housekeeper and her daughter, were assassinated in 1989. He has written many books and articles on the Theology of Liberation, including *Jesus the Liberator: a Historical-Theological Reading of Jesus of Nazareth* (1991); *Christ the Liberator: A View from the Victims* (1999); and *Where Is God? Earthquake, Terrorism, Barbarity, and Hope* (2004). He holds a doctorate in theology from the University of Frankfurt.

ROMULO TORRES SEOANE is Executive Coordinator of the Latin American Network on Debt and Development (LATINDADD). The Network has a strong popular education and grassroots focus. He is also a member of Jubilee Peru and a consultant for the Department of Solidarity of Peru's Episcopal Commission for Social Action. He has presented at and participated in many international conferences, including the 2005 Debt Conference at the G8 summit in Edinburgh, Scotland.